This succinct and to-the-point volume exemplifies the rigor, insight and originality with which David Collins continues to address the Management Guru phenomenon. It is a must for researchers and students in business and management, and for the general reader.

– **Bill Cooke,** *Chair in Strategy,*
University of York Management School, UK

Management Gurus

This book provides a concise, critical expert overview of the elite group of consultants, analysts and commentators known as 'management gurus'.

Often dismissed as lacking in substance, this volume demonstrates that gurus must be taken seriously given their impact on the world of management. Noting that the gurus are very much products of the 1980s, the book accounts for the rise of this group while challenging those who have attempted to personify – to name and acclaim – the gurus. Reviewing the research on management gurus, the book proceeds from a consideration of 'guru theory' to offer an analysis of 'the guru industry' and 'guru speak'. Building upon this analysis the book offers a critical engagement with those who have sought to understand gurus as performance artists.

Concluding with a radical agenda for future research which situates management gurus within the frame of stand-up comedy, this book will enlighten and entertain scholars across the business disciplines and beyond.

David Collins is Professor in Management at Newcastle Business School, University of Northumbria, UK. A graduate of the Universities of Glasgow, Strathclyde and Essex. He is British by birth and Scottish by the grace of God. This is his fifth book on the business of management.

State of the Art in Business Research
Series Editor: Geoffrey Wood

Recent advances in theory, methods and applied knowledge (alongside structural changes in the global economic ecosystem) have presented researchers with challenges in seeking to stay abreast of their fields and navigate new scholarly terrains.

State of the Art in Business Research presents shortform books which provide an expert map to guide readers through new and rapidly evolving areas of research. Each title will provide an overview of the area, a guide to the key literature and theories and time-saving summaries of how theory interacts with practice.

As a collection, these books provide a library of theoretical and conceptual insights, and exposure to novel research tools and applied knowledge, that aid and facilitate in defining the state of the art, as a foundation stone for a new generation of research.

Management and Organizational History
A Research Overview
Albert J. Mills, Milorad M. Novicevic

Employee Engagement
A Research Overview
Brad Shuck

Operations Management
A Research Overview
Michael A. Lewis

Management Gurus
A Research Overview
David Collins

For more information about this series, please visit: www.routledge.com

Management Gurus

A Research Overview

David Collins

LONDON AND NEW YORK

First published 2021
by Routledge
2 Park Square, Milton Park, Abingdon, Oxon OX14 4RN

and by Routledge
52 Vanderbilt Avenue, New York, NY 10017

Routledge is an imprint of the Taylor & Francis Group, an informa business

British Library Cataloguing-in-Publication Data
A catalogue record for this book is available from the British Library

Library of Congress Cataloging-in-Publication Data
A catalog record for this book has been requested

ISBN: 978-0-367-26500-7 (hbk)
ISBN: 978-0-367-52047-2 (pbk)
ISBN: 978-0-429-29708-3 (ebk)

DOI: 10.4324/9780429297083

Typeset in Times New Roman
by Apex CoVantage, LLC

Contents

1 Introduction
Aims and structure

This short, but important, chapter has been designed to introduce the aims and the structure of this little book. The chapter is important, despite its size, because it has rather a lot of work to do. Or as managers are now wont to say: This chapter must perform some 'heavy lifting'. Yet despite the fact that I understand that (as the Irish proverb has it) 'a good start is half the work', I hesitate . . . I struggle to express my core intention in a fashion that is lucid and yet robust.

The front cover, of course, suggests that this little book is about management's gurus. And this is, of course, perfectly correct . . . at one level. This text *is* concerned with the gurus of management. It aims to provide an overview of current research *and* suggestions for future research directions. Yet this bald statement does not actually amount to a promising start. And it will most certainly not take us half-way to the task that I hope to complete!

There are, after all, rather a lot of texts about 'the gurus of management' presently available in the market for management knowledge. And academic narratives, if they are to secure and sustain an audience, need to demonstrate that their focus and intent is distinctive. That is why so many scholarly works turn upon the hinges of 'currency' and 'controversy' (Collins, 2007). So let's agree shall we that this little book is *not* simply about the gurus of management?

Why am I defining this book in negative terms? Why am I making such an effort to tell you what this book is *not* concerned to examine? The answer is relatively straightforward: I fear that to do otherwise would be to indulge a number of ideas that we must now reappraise. Thus to state simply that this book is 'about the gurus of management' would be to indulge the presumption that we can readily identify an elite cadre of wise actors (*the* gurus). Furthermore, an opening statement of this form would project the understanding that such gurus deserve our veneration because through some combination of education, experience and energy (Huczynski, 1993) they have enabled those who manage our corporations, our schools and our hospitals to secure mastery of the problem of change.

For reasons that I will elaborate here, and throughout this book, I must reject these suggestions. It is, as chapter two will demonstrate, not at all clear that we can forge a general consensus as to the identity of *the* gurus of management. Nor is it obvious that the individuals identified as *the* gurus actually convey benefit to 'organisations' (as united entities). Working at a more pragmatic level it may also be useful to note that a simple declaration to the effect that this book is 'about the gurus of management' would make this text *just* another derivative work within a rather crowded market segment. Indeed a declaration of this sort would make the text you now have before you just another one of those books which casually lists and ranks both ideas and people – typically men and more often than not members of the Mormon congregation[1] – according to some under-developed and largely unarticulated notion of utility and/or popularity. And no publisher I hope is presently commissioning books of this sort!

So let us be clear: This is not *just* a(nother) book about 'the gurus of management'. A book in this form would lack novelty and currency. It would be a bore.

Yet this suggestion of *ennui* should not be taken as an indication that I am not actually interested in the broad grouping of writers and speakers who have been named and acclaimed as 'gurus' of management. I am in fact fascinated by this grouping and have devoted much of my adult life trying to come to terms with it. Why have I done this? Well, some would say I lack imagination. I protest however that I take this grouping seriously (while debating its nature and contours) because I understand that the gurus have:

- (re)shaped the essence of management thought,
- (re)defined the nature of management practice,
- altered our sense of ourselves, and through this reworking of identity have
- acted to reshape how we live, how we love and how we die.[2]

(see Ritzer, 2003[3])

For these reasons (and more) I am quite convinced that the actors, agencies and institutions which now shape our understanding of 'good' management *should* be discussed and *need to be scrutinised*. Books which focus upon *the* gurus however commit to just a proportion of this agenda. Texts on *the* gurus discuss management and managing, of course, but their central concern is not analytical nor is it critical. Instead texts on *the* gurus generate accounts of the problems of managing and organising that are subordinated to a chauvinistic desire to array and to applaud the contribution of those special individuals who are taken to be, both, wise and charismatic.

In contrast to the chauvinism which underpins so much of what has been written on management's gurus, this book seeks a broader and more critical engagement with management knowledge. Indeed this book – while taking management's gurus seriously – has been designed to allow you, the reader, to explore and to reconsider the representations of managerial work that now saturate our world. This book, therefore, seeks to provide a critical overview of research on management's gurus and suggestions for future inquiry. It seeks a deeper engagement with practices, with processes and with the people (the hewers of wood and the drawers of water)[4] variously pushed aside (or pushed under) by the problematics embodied within, and enabled by, guru theorising.

Accordingly the book is structured as follows: Chapter two offers an analysis of those texts on *the* gurus which, as we shall see, have attempted to order and array those, now, empowered to define management. This chapter will consider attempts to personify *the* gurus of management. It will suggest, however, that such attempts to name and acclaim the gurus of management are deeply flawed and distracting. Yet having criticised such attempts to order and array *the* gurus we will drop a ladder back down into the black hole which is guru personification.

Building upon the seminal work of Huczynski (1993), we will offer a consideration not of *the* gurus but of the nature and contours of guru theorising. While observing that attempts to personify the gurus of management amount to a fool's errand,[5] we will argue that we may begin to come to terms with management's gurus through an analysis of the deeper structure of ideas that bring form and (perhaps more importantly) dignity to their concerns.

In chapter three we will pause to consider the rise of the gurus. Here we will ask: Why and how do we find ourselves beholden to management's gurus? This is an important but often overlooked issue. Indeed those under the age of 40 (perhaps) may struggle to understand that there was a time, not so long ago, when the shelves of airport bookshops did not sag under the weight of texts designed, ostensibly, to make our organisations better, bigger and more competitive. But there was I assure you a simpler time when the rhythms and processes of our working lives were not shaped by notions of culture change, re-engineering and hyper-competition.

Placing guru theory (and the representations of managing and organising upon which it both builds and depends) within the turbulent decade that was the 1980s we will locate the rise of the gurus within an appropriate socio-historical context. Having established a (potted) history of the gurus and, having established the presence of 'demand-pull' factors which made the need for the resolutions proposed by guru theory apparent, we will turn to consider 'supply-side' issues. Building upon Engwall et al. (2016), we will offer a brief account of the manner in which business schools, management consultants and the business press have, together, enabled the rise of the gurus. Finally in an attempt to provide some measure of rehabilitation for the users of guru theory we will consider the typology developed by Grint (1997a, 1997b).

In chapter four we will turn our attention to those commentaries that have grown up around 'the gurus'. Here we will offer reflections on the 'guru industry'. This 'guru industry', as we shall see, has been configured to situate and to account for the different ways in which academics, journalists and, indeed, practitioners have attempted to come to terms with the gurus. In chapter five we turn to consider what, elsewhere, I have termed 'the full circuit of guru theorising' (Collins, 2019). Here we will blur the boundaries between the worlds of business and 'show business' as we offer reflections upon the seminar performances offered by management's gurus.

Greatbatch and Clark (2005), as we shall see, have suggested that academic attempts to come to terms with guru theory have been limited by a tendency to focus, narrowly, upon the books produced by/for the gurus of management. This focus upon the written word, the authors protest, has led to a failure to consider guru performance (which we will refer to as 'guru speak'). Chapter five will acknowledge the validity of this critical intervention. Yet we will argue that the 'guru speak' project is counter-productive because it is limited by problems conceptual, methodological and empirical which have not been properly scrutinised. In chapter six we build upon this critique as we signal new directions for research on management's gurus. Building upon the essence of the argument developed by Greatbatch and Clark, this final chapter will frame a new agenda for research and will suggest a new conceptualisation of the guru-as-performer which builds upon an appreciation of the dynamics of stand-up comedy.

Notes

1 This quip (it is truthfully no more than a quip) derives from Hindle (2008), who observes that there are more Mormon management gurus than there are British-born gurus!
2 This is of course particularly the case for those texts and for those authors concerned with 'self-help' and within this market segment, 'stress management', 'time management', 'self-confidence' and 'anxiety'.
3 Ritzer's work suggests that we might extend my reference to 'living, loving and dying' to include mourning. Thus Ritzer demonstrates that notions of 'organisational needs' and 'efficiency' demand that the recently bereaved limit their 'on-site' mourning at London's crematoria to no more than 15 minutes! Those who transgress this time limit are, it seems, now subject to fines that are levied upon the undertakers.
4 This is of course an allusion to the Book of Joshua 9:23. The hewers of wood and

the drawers of water are revealed as cursed in this book of the Bible. Those down-sized, delayered and de-hired in the name of 'good' management, 'good' practice or enhanced 'shareholder value' might well consider themselves to be marked in a similar manner.

5 A fool's errand may be defined as a task designed temporarily to remove/detain those who would otherwise impede purposeful endeavour. I can recall, for example, my father speaking of foolish apprentices who would be sent to a far part of the establishment where he worked in Kilmarnock to retrieve 'a long stand and a big weight' from the individual in charge of the store room. Those who worked within the storeroom it seems understood this code well, such that apprentices sent on this errand would endure 'a big wait and a long stand' before being returned to their normal place of employment!

2 Who are the gurus?

The limits of personification

Introduction

This chapter will offer a critical analysis of those texts that have sought to identify *the* gurus of management. We undertake this analysis so that we might come to recognise the chauvinism that prevails in this arena *and* the limits of personification. This chapter however is no simple exercise in debunking (Collins, 2001, 2012a). Where others would dismiss the gurus as distractions from the real business of managing, this chapter will demonstrate that these pundits are important and are, despite the critical reflections developed here, worthy of serious research.

The chapter is structured as follows: We begin with very brief reflections on the origins of the term 'management guru'. Here we will observe the existence of a dispute as regards the origin of this term. Yet having considered this dispute we will, in effect, set it aside. Instead we will consider the manner in which contemporary commentators have sought to apply and to account for this label.

Noting that casual usage of the term 'management guru' is generally associated with an attempt to name and acclaim *the* gurus we will consider the limitations of such attempts to constitute and to personify an organisational elite. Having revealed the limitations of this agenda we will consider the account of 'guru theory' developed by Huczynski (1993) and the complementary analysis offered by Kieser (1997). This alternative means of framing debate on management's gurus, as we shall see, is productive because it invites reflection not on *the* gurus but upon the deeper structure of ideas and assumptions that makes the representations of life, work, organisation and change, preferred by this elite grouping, both substantive and pressing.

Yet, having applauded the works of Kieser and Huczynski, we will nonetheless suggest that the accounts of guru theory developed by these authors are limiting because they a) tend to indulge an externalist form of analysis and b) presume that the gurus are, in a simple and conventional sense, the authors of 'their' texts. Noting the presence of 'internalist' (Grint, 1997a, 1997b) and 'translation' (Collins, 2004) based alternatives to the 'externalist' reading of guru theory, we will offer counter-points to the resonant analyses of Huczynski and Kieser before turning to consider the question of authorship.

McKenna (2016) offers a truly fascinating account of the development of two key management texts. His analysis, as we shall see, raises critical questions as to the nature of authorship. Indeed he demands that we must 'write-in' a critical appreciation of the work undertaken by ghost-writers, editors and serried ranks of 'research assistants' as we attempt to come to terms with guru theory. The chapter will then conclude with brief reflections on the ways in which this account of the nature of guru theory challenges attempts to personify *the* gurus while provoking a reconsideration of the ways and means of guru theorising.

The gurus of management

We are now so familiar with that elite cadre of commentators known as 'the gurus of management' that it is worth pausing to remind ourselves that the term, 'guru' was, until quite recently, reserved for religious figures and spiritual teachers. Indeed, dictionary compilers observe that the term 'guru' was not employed in a secular context until the mid-1960s. The 'management guru' label, however, seems to have been a still later refinement; a product of the 1980s.

In interviews, Tom Peters, who has variously been dubbed a guru, *the* guru, the Ur-guru and the Uber-guru of management (see Collins, 2007), often asserts that it was *The Economist* newspaper which should shoulder the responsibility for this refinement. Indeed, Peters suggests that it was *The Economist* which first used the term 'management guru' to describe and to account for his public representation of the business of management. Greatbatch and Clark (2005), however, offer a dissenting opinion. They suggest that the term 'management guru' was developed and first utilised by *The Sunday Times* in 1983.

This dispute as to the origins of the term 'management guru' is genuinely intriguing. Yet, beyond the specialist community which compiles and maintains dictionaries, I suggest that it really matters little who first developed and applied the term. What will become abundantly clear, however, is that while the management guru label is now in common use it remains pretty vague, fairly contentious and more than a little problematic.

Stuart Crainer (1998a) and Carol Kennedy ([1991] 1996, [1994] 1998), however, seem untroubled by such controversies. Indeed their texts appear to accept that the term 'management guru' is thoroughly complimentary and is, furthermore, rooted within practical movements and analytical

developments which allow us simply to *name and acclaim* this elite grouping of commentators.

Discussing the factors which make these commentators so special, Kennedy argues that *the* gurus of management constitute an organisational elite.
This organisational elite, she insists, is worthy of our attention because it
a) develops novel ideas and b) promotes practices that are useful and dura-
ble. There are however at least three problems with these assertions.

Firstly we might ask: If *the* gurus do indeed produce ideas that are dura-
ble why does Kennedy feel the need to produce two separate guru listings
within a three year period (see Figures 2.1 and 2.2)? And why is it that these
listings overlap only partially?

Secondly Kennedy's suggestion as to novelty is challenged, for example,
by Grint's (1994) reflections on Business Process Reengineering. Grint
argues that it is seldom possible to demonstrate that the ideas proffered by

1. John Adair	21. Philip Kotler
2. H Igor Ansoff	22. John P Kotter
3. Chris Argyris	23. Theodore Levitt
4. Chester Barnard	24. Rensis Likert
5. Meredith Belbin	25. Douglas McGregor
6. Warren Bennis	26. Abraham Maslow
7. Edward de Bono	27. Elton W Mayo
8. Alfred D Chandler	28. Henry Mintzberg
9. W Edwards Deming	29. Kenichi Ohmae
10. Peter Drucker	30. Richard T Pascale
11. Henri Fayol	31. Tom Peters and Robert H Waterman Jr
12. Gary Hamel	32. Michael Porter
13. Michael Hammer	33.Reg Revans
14. Charles Handy	34. Edgar H Schein
15. Frederick Herzberg	35. Richard J Schonberger
16. John Humble	36. E F Schumacher
17. Elliot Jaques	37. Peter M Senge
18. Joseph M Juran	38. Alfred P Sloan
19. Rosabeth Moss Kanter	39. F W Taylor
20. Robert S Kaplan and David P Norton.	40. Max Weber

Figure 2.1 The 40 management gurus as listed by Kennedy ([1991] 1996)

Adair, John	Kotter, John P
Ansoff, H Igor	Levitt, Theodore
Bartlett, Christopher A	McGregor, Douglas
Bennis, Warren	McCormack, Mark
Campbell, Andrew	Maslow, Abraham
Crosby, Philip B	Mintzberg, Henry
Deming, W Edwards	Ohmae, Kenichi
Drucker, Peter F	Pascale, Richard T
Eccles, Robert G	Peters, Tom
Fayol, Henri	Porter Michael
Ghoshal, Sumantra	Sadler, Philip
Grove, Andrew S	Schonberger, Richard J
Hammer, Michael	Schwartz, Peter
Handy, Charles	Senge, Peter
Harvey-Jones, John	Stalk George Jr
Herzberg, Frederick	Strassman, Paul A
Hofstede, Geert	Taylor, F W
Hout, Thomas M	Trompenaars, Fons
Jaques, Eliot	Waterman, Robert H Jr
Juran, Joseph M	Weber, Max
Kanter, Rosabeth M	Wendt, Henry
Kepner, Charles H and Tregoe, Benjamin B	

Figure 2.2 The 43 gurus as listed by Kennedy ([1994] 1996)

management's gurus (however constituted and arrayed) are, in fact, new. Indeed he insists that the ideas of those acclaimed as leading gurus quickly attract an audience precisely because they lack novelty.

Thirdly we would do well to acknowledge that in complex organisations, calculations as to the practical utility of an initiative will tend to be, both, multiple and contestable. For example you may wish to reflect upon the many different ways in which a 'good experience' of 'healthcare' might be constituted!

Crainer (1998a), we should concede, is altogether less concerned by claims to originality when considering the value and appeal of management's gurus. He does, however, share Kennedy's interest in durability. Thus Crainer's text highlights '50 thinkers who made management' (see Figure 2.3). Reflecting upon this select grouping, Crainer acknowledges that it is somewhat arbitrary. Indeed he acknowledges that to some extent, all guru listings could be

1. Igor Ansoff	26. Kurt Lewin
2. Chris Argyris	27. Douglas McGregor
3. Chester Barnard	28. Nicolo Machiavelli
4. Warren Bennis	29. Abraham Maslow
5. Marvin Bower	30. Konosuke Matsushita
6. Dale Carnegie	31. Elton Mayo
7. James Champy	32. Henry Mintzberg
8. Alfred Chandler	33. Akio Morita
9. W Edwards Deming	34. John Naisbitt
10. Peter Drucker	35. Kenichi Ohmae
11. Henri Fayol	36. David Packard
12. Mary Parker Follett	37. Richard Pascale
13. Henry Ford	38. Laurence J Peter
14. Harold Geneen	39. Tom Peters
15. Sumantra Ghoshal	40. Michael Porter
16. Gary Hamel	41. Edgar H Schein
17. Charles Handy	42. Peter Senge
18. Bruce Henderson	43. Alfred P Sloan
19. Frederick Herzberg	44. Frederick W Taylor
20. Geert Hofstede	45. Alvin Toffler
21. Elliot Jaques	46. Robert Townsend
22. Joseph M Juran	47. Fons Trompenaars
23. Rosabeth Moss Kanter	48. Sun-Tzu
24. Philip Kotler	49. Thomas Watson Jr
25. Ted Levitt	50. Max Weber

Figure 2.3 The 50 gurus as listed by Crainer (1998a)

accused of subjectivity, bias and error. He then demonstrates the subjectivity of his own selection by providing an appendix which contains the names of an additional 62 'thinkers with strong cases for inclusion' (265) in the main text. The presence of this appendix is not in itself problematic. Any attempt to produce a list of persons and deeds will be, inevitably, subjective.[1] What *is* problematic is that Crainer (1998a) fails to explain what it was, ultimately, that made the 62 'thinkers with strong cases for inclusion' (256) marginal to his text. There are consequently good reasons to question the calculus that underpins Crainer's final selection of *the* (50) gurus of management.

Hindle (2008) is similarly open about the difficulties associated with any attempt to produce a (portable) digest of guru theorising. Hindle who worked for *The Economist* during the early 1980s (and who was, I suspect, the individual who saddled Tom Peters with the 'management guru' moniker) acknowledges that his original intention had been to record the contributions of some 100 gurus. He confides however that he was forced to abandon this ambitious project due to a lack of space and finally settled for *just* 54 gurus (see Figure 2.4).

1. Igor Ansoff	28. Konosuke Matshusita
2. Warren Bennis	29. Elton Mayo
3. Marvin Bower	30. Douglas McGregor
4. Warren Buffett	31. Henry Mintzberg
5. Dale Carnegie	32. Akio Morita
6. Alfred Chandler	33. Ikujiro Nonaka
7. Clayton Christensen	34. Kenichi Ohmae
8. Jim Collins	35. Taiichi Ohno
9. Stephen Covey	36. Robert Owen
10. W Edwards Deming	37. C Northcote Parkinson
11. Peter Drucker	38. Richard Pascale
12. Henri Fayol	39. Laurence Peter
13. Pankaj Ghemawat	40. Tom Peters
14. Sumantra Ghoshal	41. Michael Porter
15. Frank and Lillian Gilbreth	42. C K Prahalad
16. Gary Hamel	43. Richard Rumelt
17. Michael Hammer	44. E F Schumacher
18. Charles Handy	45. Peter Senge
19. Geert Hofstede	46. Herbert Simon
20. Elliot Jaques	47. Alfred Sloan
21. Joseph Juran	48. Frederick Winslow Taylor
22. Rosabeth Moss Kanter	49. Alvin Toffler
23. Robert Kaplan and David Norton	50. Robert Townsend
24. Philip Kotler	51. Dave Ulrich
25. Theodore Levitt	52. Pierre Wack
26. James March	53. Max Weber
27. Abraham Maslow	54. William Whyte

Figure 2.4 The 54 gurus as listed by Hindle (2008)

Hindle's collection of 54 gurus and Crainer's (1998a) collection of 50 key thinkers raise some interesting if seldom examined issues. We might, for example, do well to note that these listings of *the* gurus make 'fellow travellers' of individuals whom scholars of organisation studies would not generally consider possessing very much in common at all. Beyond a broad interest in matters organisational, for example, just what is it that makes bed-fellows of Max Weber's cautious, academic sociology and Taylor's 'industrial engineering'?

The failure either to address or to respond to issues of this sort raises, I suggest, some pretty fundamental issues concerning our ability to order and array *the* gurus of management in any useful of meaningful sense. This line of criticism, however, should not be taken as implying that the works of Hindle, Kennedy and Crainer are without merit. Hindle, as we shall see, offers very useful insights on the volatility of guru careers and upon the manner in which guru theories are received within the broad community that is concerned with managerial matters.

Commenting on the process that whittled his century of commentators into a more manageable number, Hindle (2008: 1) highlights the presence of an 'A-list' of management's gurus. Thus he confides:

> The final selection of ideas and gurus included here was inevitably a personal one. There are 54 gurus in this book, but there could as easily be 154. A small band of names appears in virtually all such lists – a band that is more or less confined to what can be called the 'Famous Five': Peter Drucker, Douglas McGregor, Michael Porter, Alfred Sloan and Frederick Winslow Taylor.

Working together, Des Dearlove and Stuart Crainer have, in a similar fashion, attempted to identify the very cream of guru theorising. Building upon periodic surveys which rank the gurus according to their 'influence', Dearlove and Crainer now produce regular league tables of *the* gurus. The methodology underpinning this ranking exercise is somewhat vague. Nonetheless it would be accurate to observe that the 2009 listing, to take but one example, builds (however loosely) upon a survey of 3,500 'people' *and* a panel of 'experts' of indeterminate size (see Figure 2.5). This periodic survey, despite its rather obvious methodological flaws, is interesting for at least four reasons. Firstly it is routinely published by *Forbes* and so enjoys some standing within the business and finance communities. Secondly its annual launch takes place at a swanky, high-price gala event. The presence of this event on the calendar is, I suggest, significant because it demonstrates that the contours of this industry and the boundaries of 'popular management' are rather more extensive and altogether more complex than we generally acknowledge (see Collins, 2016).

Top 10 Ranking (2009)	Ranking in 2007 Survey
10. Gary Hamel	05
09. Philip Kotler	11
08. Richard Branson	09
07. Bill Gates	02
06. Muhammad Yunus	*New Entrant*
05. W Chan Kim and Reneé Mauborgne	06
04. Steve Jobs	29
03. Paul Krugman	*New Entrant*
02. Malcolm Gladwell	18
01. C K Prahalad	01

Top 10 Ranking (2017)
10. Rita McGrath
09. Richard D'Aventi
08. Adam Grant
07. Alexander Osterwalder and Yves Pigneur
06. Marshall Goldsmith
05. Michael Porter
04. W Chan Kim and Reneé Mauborgne
03. Clayton Christensen
02. Don Tapscott
01. Roger Martin

Figure 2.5 The 'Top 10 Most Influential Gurus' in 2009 and 2017 according to *Forbes*

Source: For 2009 and 2007 figures see www.forbes.com/2009/10/13/influential-business-thinkers-leadership-thought-leaders-gurus_slide.html#29d89a3264af

For 2017 figures see www.forbes.com/sites/jeffkaulfin/2017/11/14/the-worlds-most-influential-business-thinkers-2017/#7a7b7cf35ec4

Thirdly, and perhaps more importantly for the purposes of this chapter, the Dearlove-Crainer listing creates what amounts to 'hit parade' of guru theorising which suggests that individual gurus tend to rise and fall in the public consciousness. Fourthly the 'famous five' acknowledged by Hindle and the 'top 10' routinely arrayed within the covers of *Forbes* are intriguing because they omit the individual whom, I suggest, represents the very archetype of the modern management guru: Tom Peters (see Collins, 2007). Accounting for this omission from the 'famous five', Hindle notes that in 2003 the *Harvard Business Review* (HBR) invited a number of key business thinkers to nominate their favourite guru. Peter Drucker, he tells us, came top of the list, James March was second and Tom Peters featured not at all.

The exclusion of Tom Peters from the listings produced by HBR and *Forbes* merits further analysis and reflection but it is, perhaps, not so surprising as Hindle would have us believe. Indeed the omission of Peters from the Harvard 'famous five' and from the 'top 10' listings periodically reproduced by *Forbes* may be readily explained in methodological terms. For example we might venture that the omission of Peters from these listings is more a product of the populations surveyed than a true index of this individual's standing in the field of management knowledge. Equally we might suggest that the omission of Tom Peters could be a product of 'social reporting' whereby respondents choose to disguise their preferences and instead report actions, choices and orientations that reflect societal predilections and/or the perceived inclinations of the researcher. In this regard, Tom Peters' exclusion from the 'famous five' may be a product of those processes which cause dinner party guests to profess a love of the books of Gabriel Garcia Marquez whilst (and because) they secretly prefer films featuring the comic stylings of Adam Sandler. Thus we might suggest that it is Tom Peters' market success and the common prejudice which equates popularity with low-brow vulgarity (Collins, 2012b) which has encouraged the readers of HBR (and the respondents to the Crainer-Dearlove survey) to represent their preferences in a manner that denies Peters his place in the pantheon.

Rigby (2011), who has also prepared a text concerned with management ideas and business practices, makes common purpose with Crainer (1998a) and with Hindle (2008) insofar as he also acknowledges the difficulties associated with any attempt to identify an elite of management studies. Rigby deals with this issue however in an interesting manner: He attempts to side-step the problem. Thus Rigby draws our attention not to gurus, but rather more vaguely to 28 'business thinkers' (see Figure 2.6) who have acted as 'game changers', exercising 'a significant and lasting effect on the world of business and sometimes even the world' (2).

Rigby's approach to this cataloguing exercise is, we should acknowledge, refreshing. Despite being shorter than the other texts noted here, Rigby's book contains more women and produces a broader and more eclectic catalogue of 'thinkers'.

Yet despite his *legerdemain* Rigby is unable to evade the perils which accompany any attempt to separate one section of the community from another. Thus Rigby's listing of 'business thinkers', while distinctive, remains

1. Steve Jobs	15. Bill Gates
2. Richard Branson	16. David Ogilvy
3. Warren Buffett	17. Meg Whitman
4. Jeff Bezos	18. Mark Zuckerberg
5. The Google Duo (Sergey Brin and Larry Page)	19. Howard Schultz
6. Sir Tim Berners-Lee	20. Jack Welch
7. Anita Roddick	21. Michael Dell
8. Ray Kroc	22. Tom Peters! (sic)
9. Rupert Murdoch	23. Ricardo Semler
10. Peter Drucker	24. Herb Kelleher
11. Ingvar Kampard	25. Andy Grove
12. Oprah (sic)	26. Roman Abrahamovich
13. Sam Walton	27. George Soros
14. Mary Kay Ash	28. Akio Morita

Figure 2.6 The 28 'game-changing' business thinkers listed by Rigby (2011)

somewhat arbitrary and is, at times, confusing. The nature of the contribution made by Berners-Lee to the practice of management, for example, escapes me! Furthermore Rigby's inclusion of Ricardo Semler surely challenges the generally accepted definition of 'game changers' in this context.

Ricardo Semler (1994) published *Maverick* in the early 1990s. This text, we should acknowledge, sold well and did attract favourable comment around this time. Indeed, we should concede that Semler's (espoused) practices and his preferred approach to the management of business enterprises encouraged many to talk of 'empowerment'. Furthermore we should acknowledge that Semler did have something interesting to say about work-life balance insofar has he suggested that managers, employees and owners might usefully spend extended periods away from the workplace. More than 25 years from the publication of *Maverick*, however, it is far from clear that Semler's personal contribution has, in any meaningful sense, altered the game that is managing. It is, however, worth observing that Tom Peters can certainly voice this claim because he has, through his books and lectures, changed the ways in which people think about management, talk about management and, when all is said done, act managerially (Collins, 2007).

Of course it would also be appropriate to observe that mere mention of the name Tom Peters tends to excite and polarise opinion. Nevertheless – like him or loathe him – it is plain that Tom Peters *entered and altered the market for management knowledge* in the early 1980s. Indeed, it would not be an exaggeration to suggest that (deliberately or otherwise) Tom Peters crafted, in his own image, the ideal of the management guru which now haunts our attempts to personify this section of the commentariat. Furthermore, we should acknowledge that Peters has (in the company of just a handful of others) sustained a prominent position within the market segment which he planted and propagated almost 40 years ago. In this regard we might venture the opinion that Tom Peters, despite the prejudices of those who contribute to guru listings, can claim to be not just *a* guru but *the* guru of management.

This recognition of Peters' status and influence however should not be taken as an unalloyed celebration of his work. Nor should it be taken as offering unconditional support for the influence that management's gurus (whether or not they appear in the 'famous five') have had upon the practice of management. Reflecting upon this point, Jackson and Carter suggest that anyone who understands the origins of the term 'guru' *should* choose to oppose its application within the field of business and management. Commenting upon the origins of this term they observe:

> The word 'guru' means a spiritual leader, and it derives from the Sanskrit word for venerable. 'Venerable' means worthy of worship, and its Latin origins are connected with Venus, the goddess of love: we should worship our gurus as fountains of love for us.
>
> (Jackson and Carter, 1998: 153–154)

Pio (2007: 184) offers a similar analysis. She notes:

> The Sanskrit word *guru* is derived from *gu*, meaning darkness, and *ru*, meaning light or the removal of the darkness of ignorance through enlightenment. The guru is expected to live up to what he or she preaches. The guru is also seen as the bridge between the individual and god and a channel for divine grace.

Recognising the spiritual origins of the term, Jackson and Carter simply refuse to countenance the suggestion that those who have, in recent years, acted to reshape the business of management actually spread enlightenment, and so, deserve our veneration. Pattison (1997) recognises the power of this sentiment. Yet he suggests that the term 'guru' has utility in this context because it offers insights into the ways in which these actors secure and solidify their representations of the world. Thus Pattison argues that the management guru label might be retained, even by archly critical scholars, because it highlights the manner in which those commentators who form the leading edge of popular management are able to shape how we think, feel and act. Expanding upon this point, Pattison suggests that the gurus of management acquire and sustain followers in a fashion that is similar to that commonly employed by religious preachers and evangelists. Thus Pattison argues that gurus (secular and otherwise) act to threaten our sense of self and in so doing promise to provide – if not redemption – then at least a release from our more pressing problems and dilemmas (see also Jackson, 1996, 2001). Offering a concrete example of this more general process, Pattison suggests that Tom Peters' second work, produced in concert with Nancy Austin (Peters and Austin, 1985), amounts to a secular re-telling of the story of Noah and the flood and, like this biblical tale, promises salvation to those who are prepared to embrace what we might now term *the rapture of business excellence*.

Greatbatch and Clark (2005) dispute this, however. They suggest that the guru label is, despite its common currency, inappropriate because there is no evidence to suggest that those who read guru texts or who listen to what these individuals have to say about the business of management actually undergo a conversion experience. This is an interesting position but it is far from persuasive. Indeed two objections may be voiced.

Firstly to suggest that practitioners of management have failed 'to convert' to the philosophies of management's gurus is surely to overlook the extent to which managers and politicians of all hues do, now, think and speak about 'culture change', 'empowerment' and 'quality' precisely because of their gurus. Secondly I suggest that we do not need to establish that those who encounter management's gurus emerge as zealots – as converts fired with new and enduring passions in order to demonstrate that the term has utility in this context.

Commenting upon the revivalist preacher Billy Graham's visit to Scotland in 1955, Roy (2013: 180) invites us to reconsider the manner in which we conceive such evangelical missionary work. Roy readily affirms Graham's ability to attract an audience: Two-and-a-half million people (one half of Scotland's population), he tells us, attended Graham's events in Glasgow or watched the proceedings on relayed broadcasts. Yet despite this staggering level of engagement, Roy notes the general absence of converts moved to a new life in Christ. He notes that, despite Graham's mission of 1955, and despite a subsequent visit in the late 1980s, membership of the Church of Scotland has continued to decline from its mid-1950s peak of 37% of the adult Scottish population to its present-day standing of less than 9%. Furthermore, Roy observes that the reaction of Scotland's 500,000 Roman Catholics to Graham's mission then (and to subsequent visitations) was 'negligible'. Given Scotland's experience of Graham's evangelism, it seems sensible to suggest that Greatbatch and Clark (2005) have unrealistic expectations of religious evangelists and consequently set the bar too high for the secularised gurus of management.

Is it possible to navigate a route through (and out of) the disputed territory revealed through our critical engagement with *the* gurus and with the listings and hit parades developed to catalogue these individuals? Yes, I believe it is.

My position is as follows: Most sensible commentators, I suggest, would tend to concede the existence of an 'A-list' of managerial commentators who have enjoyed popular acclaim and volume sales because they have, through writing and public speaking, constructed an account of the business of management that threatens and redeems managerial identities. The contents of this 'A-list' will vary geographically (see Cooke et al., 2012) and, I suspect, with your date of birth.[2] Nonetheless it seems sensible to suggest that the likes of Tom Peters (Peters and Waterman, 1982), Peter Drucker (see Drucker, [1955] 2007), Richard Pascale (Pascale and Athos, 1981), Steve Jobs (see Isaacson, 2011), Richard Branson (1998), Rosabeth Moss Kanter (1989), Anita Roddick (1991, 2005) and (perhaps) Lee Iacocca (see Iacocca and Novak, 1984; Iacocca and Kleinfield, 1988) would *make the list*. And beyond this observation, frankly, I have no real or sustained interest in guru personification and would certainly not seek to impose a personal top 10, top 50 or even a top 100 upon anyone else. But it would be wrong to conclude our reflections on this note because, as we shall see, Huczysnki (1993) offers an account of 'guru theory' which can liberate us from the problems of *listeria*.

Guru theory

Huczynski (1993) observes that managers have been able to purchase laudatory books on the practice of management since at least the 1900s. Indeed it is worth observing that some writers from this period – Dale Carnegie, Mary Parker Follett, FW Taylor and Henri Fayol[3] – appear on the guru listings reproduced in this chapter. Furthermore we would do well to note that at least one writer from an earlier period – Robert Owen – also features on the guru listings reproduced here. Nevertheless, Huczynski reminds us that the growth of a mass market in 'popular management', and the related rise of management's gurus, are very much products of the 1980s.

Yet unlike other analysts who have sought to personify the gurus, Huczynski actually warns us against any attempt to reduce management's gurus to a compact or regimented collective. Indeed he argues that when we make reference to *the* gurus we are actually highlighting the existence of a diverse grouping and the presence of a rather loose bundle of ideas. Nonetheless Huczynski does suggest that those who have been labelled as management's gurus tend to belong to one of three broad classes of commentator: the academic guru, the consultant guru and the hero-manager. Reflecting upon the ways in which these individuals derive their authority and appeal, Huczynski argues that the academic and consultant gurus tend to highlight their education and training whereas the hero-managers trade more upon their experience.

Suddaby and Greenwood (2001), however, question this categorisation. They suggest that it fails to capture the complexity of the CVs which these actors possess. At one level, of course, this is fair criticism. Tom Peters, who I insist remains among the leading 'consultant gurus', holds advanced degrees in civil engineering and in management. He is, consequently, *at least* as qualified as his academic counterparts. Likewise the modern executives who run our corporations and who are, from time to time, celebrated as 'hero-managers' are, thanks to a revolution in management education (see Bryan, 2009), often qualified to a very high standard nowadays. Yet, despite (increasing) similarities in background and educational attainment, Huczynski remains correct in his assertion that the gurus tend to speak in different registers such that the consultant and academic gurus *do* generally play upon their training whereas the 'hero-managers' prefer to trade upon their experience and upon their intrinsic leadership capabilities.

Reflecting upon the marketability of these gurus, Hindle (2008) reminds us that the career prospects of these commentators are far from assured. Gurus are, in effect, brands. And the history of marketing teaches us that most attempts to secure a branded identity culminate in failure. Thus Hindle observes that, aside from the 'famous five' who have sustained prominent positions in the market for management knowledge, most of those who have been dubbed 'management gurus' tend to flourish briefly and then fade (sometimes ignominiously) from public life.[4] Huczynski (1993), I suspect, would tend to accept this account of the career-path of management's gurus but would add the caveat that while *gurus* may well come and go, *guru theory* endures.

Outlining the nature and character of 'guru theory', Huczynski (1993: 38) concedes that

> the term 'guru theory' is used as a convenient label to refer to [the] different contributions that have been so influential [since the 1980s]. The label encompasses a rag-bag of prescriptions which include the importance of innovation, more teamwork, more empowerment of the individual, more employee participation, fewer levels of hierarchy and less bureaucratization.

Huczynski insists however that there is a deeper structure of orientations and representations which draws the strings of this 'rag-bag' together. Indeed he suggests that modern guru theory develops and retains an audience by focusing upon presentation and by cultivating an ideological focus which serves to enhance the rights and privileges of management. Fleshing out this point,

Huczynski suggests that what is often reduced to 'guru theory' might more usefully be conceived as a family of ideas. Tracing the genealogy of this family Huczynski suggests that it exhibits three common, core traits and, within these traits, 12 interdependent, complementary and overlapping features. Guru theory, therefore, articulates an understanding of the world of work which is:

1   Readily communicable through acronyms, alliteration or slogans. For example the 3Cs of business process reengineering (Hammer, 1990) and the McKinsey 7-S framework, which underpins both, *In Search of Excellence* (Peters and Waterman, 1982) and *The Art of Japanese Management* (Pascale and Athos, 1981) spring readily to mind.
2   Focused upon the presumed capacity which leaders have to change the conduct of others.
3   Happy to assert that human thoughts and feelings are similarly malleable in the hands of the skilled leaders lauded at point 2.

Exploring the second trait said to typify guru theorising, Huczynski suggests that successful representations of managerial work have been designed to enhance the status of the intended purchaser. Marketable representations of managerial work he suggests:

4   Provide legitimation and self-affirmation for those engaged in managerial work. In other words, guru theory indulges the presumption that managers are truly special, genuinely heroic.
5   Build upon a unitary account of managerial work which suggests that there is no room for meaningful dissent with respect to organisational ends or indeed the means used to secure these goals (Fox, 1985).
6   Allow modifications which enable managers a) to tailor the model to local problems and contingencies and, in so doing, allow practitioners to b) voice the suggestion that they have usefully and meaningfully acted on their own initiative.
7   Focus upon 'leadership' and in so doing suggest that colleagues will volunteer their support even to the point of altruism.

Examining the third trait, Huczynski focuses, unsurprisingly, on practical application. Thus he argues that successful forms of guru theory:

8   Promise control over market conditions otherwise notable for their volatility.
9   Outline a limited number of steps that, in execution, will deliver useful, planned change (see Collins, 1998 for an account of *n*-step guides).
10 Suggest that the idea, tool or initiative enjoys universal applicability.

11 Carry authorisation or proof but not in the traditional academic or empirical sense. Commenting upon this, Lischinsky (2008) observes that popular management ideas rarely build upon original empirical research but depend instead upon 'persuasive examples'.
12 Has ready applicability and can be utilised without special tools or knowledge.

Kieser (1997) offers a similar 10-point analysis of guru rhetoric but adds an important dimension not addressed by Huczynski. Thus Kieser observes that gurus need luck! Discussing this issue, Collins (2007) offers confirmation of the role which luck as regards good timing can play in the market for guru ideas. Analysing Tom Peters' (1987) *Thriving on Chaos*, Collins suggests that in any half-way rational world the book-buying public would have rejected what is, in truth, a rather under-developed, unwieldy and uninviting text. Yet Collins notes that Tom Peters had the very good fortune to launch his text on 'Black Monday', October 19, 1987 – a day which, because it brought chaos to global financial markets, resonated with Peters' core theme.

Resonant explanations and their alternatives

Huczynski's 12-point distillation of the essence of guru theory is often referred to as a 'resonant' (Grint, 1994) or 'externalist' (Grint, 1997a, 1997b; Collins, 2000) form of analysis because it suggests that the content of guru ideas varies with context. Barley and Kunda (1992) seem to accept this but add the disclaimer that management fashions vary cyclically and move – broadly speaking – in relation to business conditions. Reflecting upon the changes which typify the business cycle, Barley and Kunda suggest that the form of guru theory developed, for example, during economic boom periods will carry little real resonance as economies enter recession. Thus Barley and Kunda observe that when profitability is high, product markets are buoyant and labour markets are tight, practitioners will be attracted to ideas which are inclined to view the central problems of management in terms of 'commitment', 'satisfaction' and 'staff retention'. Conversely they suggest that during recessionary periods managers will be more troubled by the need to secure cost-savings and, consequently, will be attracted to those representations that index these concerns.

Resonant or externalist readings, it would be fair to say, have tended to dominate our understanding of guru theory. It is worth noting therefore that Grint (1997a, 1997b) has developed a complementary account of guru theorising which reminds us of the significance of socio-economic processes *within* business organisations. This alternative, 'internalist' account of guru theorising recognises the broad appeal of the externalist narrative, yet insists that it would be wrong to suggest that we can simply locate management knowledge as a variable, rooted in and moving with, factors that remain external to the organisation. Thus Grint suggest that guru theory reflects and enables political actions and personal agendas *within* organisations. Such internalist renderings of guru theory, we should note, have both positive and more negative connotations for our appreciation of management practitioners.

On the plus side, the internalist account of guru theorising locates practitioners as situated, choice-making actors and so pushes back against those who would tend to suggest that managers are somehow cultural dopes who have been duped into using empty, faddish ideas (see Collins, 2001, 2012a). On the negative side of the equation, however, internalist accounts suggest that practitioners may be attracted to forms of guru theorising which reflect and project their own, narrow, personal ambitions regardless of whether these reflect the unitary organisational goals (Fox, 1985) that guru theory must construct and applaud. Internalist accounts of guru theory therefore remind us a) that organisations are complex, political systems and b) that managerial and other actors – despite the presence of TINA[5] (Collins and McCartney, 2010) – remain capable of exercising discretion.

More recent attempts to consider both the appeal of management's gurus and the operationalisation of 'guru theory' have highlighted the significance of 'translation'. Reflecting upon the catalogue of heroic assumptions required to operationalise the fad motif, a number of authors have suggested that management practitioners are altogether more thoughtful, more innovative and, yes, more devious than the casual deployment of this labelling device might suggest. Cole (1999), in his analysis of the American adoption of 'quality management', for example, suggests that 'quality fads' have both a history and a context. In combination, he avers, these factors undermine the suggestion that guru theory is simply diffused amongst a population given to mindless imitation. Thus Cole argues that the adoption of guru theory is built around the active translation of concepts and practices. Taking this point a step further, Giroux (2006) suggests that the adoption of guru theory turns upon local processes of adaptation which need to be invoked in order to convert these abstract and generalised representations into practical endeavours. Collins (2004) echoes this but adds that the utilisation of guru theory develops 'paragrammatically' because practitioners seldom enjoy access to all the resources that their gurus suggest will be required for full and effective implementation.

These reflections upon the nature of guru theory and its application facilitate the development of a non-destructive form of analysis which, because it recognises the localised incentives associated with guru theory, takes the users of such representations seriously as utility-seeking actors. And yet a blind spot remains. In an episode of silence, those who have written on the gurus of management tend to indulge the belief that these commentators are, in a true and meaningful sense, the authors of guru theory. This, as we shall see next, is a presumption worthy of further scrutiny.

Who writes this stuff?

So far, and partly for reasons of legibility, I have written about the gurus and guru theory *as if* these individuals (and partnerships) are clearly and simply 'the authors' of their books; the sole architects of the moral universes they would craft in our names. This choice of expression improves the flow of the text but it is, nonetheless, misleading for it is plain that many of the texts produced on the business of management, and published under covers which assert that our leading hero-managers (for example) have a talent for autobiography, have in fact been ghost-written. For example Lee Iacocca, former head of Chrysler, required the assistance of William Novak (Iacocca and Novak, 1984) when he was contracted to produce a book about his life and career. Furthermore, it is worth noting that Iacocca's second book on management and politics was produced with the assistance of Sonny Klein-feld (Iacocca and Kleinfeld, 1988). Such writing partnerships, we should note are far from exceptional in the world of the 'hero manager' (see for example Geneen and Moscow, 1986; Kiam, 1988;[6] Dunlap and Andelman, 1997; Welch and Byrne, 2001). Indeed it is worth observing that Crainer (1998b; see also Anonymous, 1999) who has, himself, acted as research assistant for Tom Peters, gleefully highlights the extent to which similarities in the writings of the gurus arise because these texts are, in fact, the products of a small collection of jobbing ghost-writers.

McKenna (2016) acknowledges the prevalence of ghost-writing within the popular management segment of the publishing industry, yet he suggests that criticisms of the practice of ghost-writing, such as that voiced by Crainer, tend to miss the point. Thus McKenna suggests that using the fact of ghost-writing to attack the capability and credibility of the gurus misunderstands, and so, misrepresents, the very nature of authorship. It may be helpful to explore this issue through a consideration of the work of Tom Peters.

Tom Peters, *uber* guru of management, insists that he is, unlike many of his contemporaries, the true author of his books. I make similar protests although I do not feel the need to question the integrity of my colleagues! There are, however, strong reasons to challenge the claim voiced by Peters and there are, if I am truthful, pretty good reasons to challenge my own assertion. This, I should say, is not the moment when I 'out' myself as a serial plagiarist. It is, however, that point in my career when I have the maturity to acknowledge that while every word in the texts I have written (quotations aside of course) is truly *mine own*, I have, throughout my career, depended upon the insights of academic colleagues, family members and reviewers. In addition I have depended upon the advice offered by the editors of academic journals and by my publishers as I have toiled to secure publication of my books and articles. Given this it is, I suggest, useful to observe that in this book as in all my others works I am the sole author of a joint enterprise!

Despite the protestations of Tom Peters much the same could be said of this man's works. For example, in *The Pursuit of Wow* (Peters, 1994), Peters draws attention to the assistance rendered by Donna Carpenter, Tom Richman and Sebastian Stuart. In addition, Peters observes that Sebastian Stuart deserves further plaudits because it was he who designed the lay-out of the book. Despite statements to the contrary therefore it seems sensible to suggest that, like me, Peters leans heavily upon the words and advice of others as he toils to develop his books. The key difference between my approach and experience and that of Peters, I suggest, turns upon the fact that he employs ranks of 'research assistants' who toil to pen company profiles and reports many of which he reproduces *verbatim* within that which he claims are his *solely-authored* works (see Crainer, 1997).

Delving more fully into the historical construction of management knowledge, McKenna (2016) extends the analysis I have outlined above and in so doing invites us to acknowledge the manner in which ghost-writers have acted to constitute our understanding of the very essence of the business of management. Taking the text *My Years with General Motors* (Sloan et al., 1965) as his example, McKenna suggests that McDonald's work on what appears to be an auto-biography is significant and merits further academic reflection. Indeed, McKenna notes that until McDonald set pen to paper on the story of Sloan's stewardship of General Motors, managers and analysts had *spoken* of 'business policy' and did not in fact begin to *think* of 'strategic management' until McDonald had coined the term!

McKenna also draws our attention to the fact that General Motors had attempted to block publication because they feared that the book's revelations would lead to 'anti-trust' action against the company. This court case and its outcome (the book was of course cleared for publication), McKenna suggests, is significant because it allows us to understand why Chandler's (1962) now classic account of strategic management was able to ignore the issue of 'anti-trust'. Reflecting upon these issues, McKenna demands that we acknowledge that it was McDonald who named the field of 'strategic management'. In addition he observes that through the legal action which he pursued against General Motors, McDonald provided clarity on the issue of 'anti-trust' regulation and in so doing effectively constituted the core problematics which shape the academic consideration of strategic management to this day.

Turning his attention to publishers and editors, McKenna also draws our attention to the active roles which these agencies and actors perform in the fields of business publishing and 'popular management'. Thus McKenna notes that, at a late stage of production, Chandler's editor intervened and in suggesting a change to the title of the book acted to ensure that structure would forever more follow strategy!

As we review and re-consider gurus and guru theory we would do well to take account of the influence which publishers, editors and ghost-writers exert. To do otherwise is a) to collapse the fields of 'popular management' and guru theorising, b) to ignore the commercial pressures which shape our understanding of the problems and processes of management, c) to misunderstand the nature of authorship and d) to under-estimate the manner in which the rise of popular management required broader institutional change within the fields of consulting, education and publishing.

In our next chapter we will offer a fuller consideration of these topics as we attempt to explain and account for the rise of management's gurus.

Concluding comments

This chapter has offered critical reflections on the gurus of management. We have suggested that attempts to order and array the gurus are unproductive and are based upon an unexamined conviction that the gurus are a) wise and are b) truly worthy of our veneration because they have c) produced innovations that are genuinely new and sustainable over time. Challenging these assertions we have nonetheless suggested that the gurus *should not* be dismissed and *do deserve to be made the subject of academic research* because they have acted to alter how we think about management and how we act when we wish to appear 'managerial'.

In an attempt to free ourselves from *listeria* and from related attempts to personify the gurus, we have built upon the works of Huczynski (1993) and Kieser (1997). Using Huczynski's pioneering analysis, we have encouraged reflection on the underlying ideas and orientations which bring meaning and substance to the pronouncements of those said to be gurus.

In preparation for our next chapter, we have offered initial reflections upon ghost-writing and, more generally, upon the question of authorship. We now turn to consider the factors enabling the rise of the gurus.

Notes

1 Baring-Gould (1914) produced the 16-volume *Lives of the Saints*. It is clear that unlike Hindle (2008) and Crainer (1998a), Baring-Gould was not particularly constrained by space considerations. Yet he prefaces the first volume with the following admission: 'In writing the lives of the Saints, I have used my discretion

. . . in relating only those miracles which are most remarkable, either for being fairly well authenticated, of for their beauty or quaintness, or because they are represented in art, and are therefore of interest to the archaeologist. That errors in judgement, and historical inaccuracies, have crept into this volume, and may find their way into those that succeed, is, I fear inevitable' (vii). Some level of subjectivity will inevitably apply to any attempt to separate one class of commentators from another. The fact that this issue a) exists, b) is commonly understood and yet c) not adequately examined by those who have produced listings of *the* gurus, leads me to reject those attempts which have been made to personify – to name and acclaim management's gurus.

2 My loose listing of those I take to be significant commentators, albeit couched in suspicion and subject to qualification, contains individuals such as Victor Kiam, Al Dunlap and Harold Geneen, which, I acknowledge, is very much a product of my year of birth. Many of my contemporaries and most younger readers may simply not recognise these men . . . at all!

3 In an attempt to keep this work short and legible, I have taken the decision to limit unnecessary referencing. I accept that this will unsettle and/or upset some readers.

4 The 'guru career' of Al Dunlap, who attempted to persuade the American public that his surname might be used as a verb for the radical form of organisational change which he brought to corporations, offers a useful challenge to those who offer unalloyed celebrations of *the* gurus of management. Dunlap, who was lauded as 'Rambo in pinstripes' and who rejoiced in the *nom du guerre* 'Chainsaw Al', was celebrated as a turnaround specialist who released shareholder benefits through radical downsizing and delayering (the euphemisms for dismissing workers, we should note, vary over time). Later, however, it was revealed that Dunlap's career was based upon a series of elaborate frauds. An accounting scandal involving his management of Sunbeam Products (which came to light in 1998) brought his putative guru career to an ignominious and overdue conclusion when he was sacked by the company. Further investigations undertaken by the Securities and Exchange Commission (SEC) suggested that Dunlap had been guilty of similar misconduct during his employment with Scott Paper. Dunlap was investigated by the US Department of Justice but no criminal charges were filed. He was, however, banned from serving as an officer or director of any public company and paid $500,000 to settle the SEC's case against him. A lawsuit undertaken by the shareholders of Sunbeam (which never recovered from Dunlap's tenure and was forced into bankruptcy in 2002) was settled in that same year when Dunlap agreed to pay $15 million. Dunlap died on January 25, 2019 with an estimated net worth of $100 million.

5 The acronym TINA stands for 'there is no alternative'. Much of guru theory proceeds on the assertion that – given 'new competitive imperatives' – organisations and their managers have no alternative but to accept 'the new reality' they face and 'embrace the challenge of change'. Reflections upon the active consumption/translation of guru theory suggest that this rhetorical imperative is inaccurate insofar as the users of guru theory routinely evade or reconstruct the competitive conditions that are said to act with imperative force.

6 Kiam, it is worth noting, does not credit his ghost-writer on the cover of his work or on the copyright notice. In a secondary dedication, however, he concedes that Dick Lally helped him to organise his thoughts and to get these down on paper. To me this suggests that Lally either edited Kiam's text or, what I believe to be more likely, actually produced the book in his name.

3 The rise of the gurus of management

Introduction

This chapter considers the rise of management's gurus. We will suggest that the gurus introduced in chapters one and two must be regarded as products of the 1980s and need to be located within the socio-economic context of that turbulent decade. Yet, where others are inclined to recount the rise of the gurus as a moment in history formed by 'a few great men',[1] we will argue that it took a network to deliver guru theory to the masses. Indeed, we will suggest that the emergence of these networked relationships is particularly interesting because, as it developed, it challenged and strained the mores of the consulting industry.

We begin by noting the rise of that sub-set of the publishing industry known as 'popular management' (Rüling, 2005). One way to gauge the growth of popular management and within this the rise of management's gurus is to consider the book buying habits of the general public. It is instructive to note therefore that until the early 1980s the non-fiction 'best sellers' lists in the US and the UK were dominated by books which documented the lives of celebrities (see for example Niven, 1971); by investigative journalism that probed the misdeeds of the business and political classes (see for example Sampson, 1973, [1975] 1991, 1977; Woodward and Bernstein, 1974); and by manuals which offered advice on sex, health and nutrition (see for example, Comfort, 1972; Fixx, 1977).

Since the 1980s, however, popular management texts (texts designed to advance and applaud the practice of management) have attracted a significant audience and have, consequently, figured very prominently in the listings published by newspapers such as *The Economist*, *The New York Times* and *The Times* (of London). Commenting on the rapid growth of this market segment, Pagel and Westerfelhaus (2005) note that by 1991 there were already 1,421 'popular management' titles available in the US. Furthermore, the authors observe that a decade later the US consumer could choose from some 5,023 popular management titles, which collectively generated $938.3 million in sales revenue. Crainer (1997: 199), however, suggests that this calculation may seriously under-estimate the market for popular management. Thus Crainer observes that by the mid-1990s the leading gurus were being paid $953 million for their speaking engagements alone. There are therefore good reasons to believe that the popular management segment of the publishing industry is not just a billion dollar marketplace but a multi-billion dollar forum.

The size and success of this market today, however, should not blind us to the fact that, viewed from the 1980s, the growth of popular management was fairly unlikely and indeed largely unexpected. In an attempt to explain this surprising shift and in so doing to offer some explanation for the success of 'popular management', this chapter will offer a critical analysis of the (unlikely) rise of the gurus. In our next section, therefore, we will offer what might be termed 'an archaeology of the excellence project'. We select the excellence project as the vehicle for our analytical review largely because the text *In Search of Management* launched the popular management segment of the publishing industry and in so doing became the exemplar of guru theorising that prevails to the present day.

In the third section we will return to a theme which we introduced towards the end of chapter two. Thus our third section will offer reflections on the changing face of the publishing industry. Building upon the analyses of Crainer (1997, 1998b) and Clark (2004), we will draw directly upon the work of Engwall et al. (2016) as we consider the manner in which commercial influences in the field of consulting and structural changes within the publishing industry have enabled the rise of the gurus.

In our fourth section we offer reflections upon the motives of those who consume guru theory. Too often, commentaries on management's gurus proceed from the assertion that the consumers of guru theory are either duped or just plain dopy (Collins, 2001, 2004, 2012a). Here we will challenge this blanket dismissal of the intellectual capabilities of those who would manage with and though guru theory. Thus we will consider Grint's (1997a, 1997b) reflections before concluding with brief comments designed as a bridge to chapter four, which will consider the 'guru industry'.

An archaeology of excellence

In Search of Excellence (Peters and Waterman, 1982), a book co-authored by Tom Peters and Bob Waterman in terms of its content, tone and, not least, sales, deserves to be recognised as the prototype of modern guru theorising (Collins, 2007; Kociatkiewicz and Kostera, 2016). In this section we will offer reflections upon the manner in which this prototype became the archetype for guru theory.

Discussing the genesis of *In Search of Excellence*, Crainer (1997) suggests that this book developed as Tom Peters' then employers, the consulting firm McKinsey and Co, sought to defend their company's market position and reputation against two key competitors: the Boston Consulting Group and Bain and Co.

In the early 1970s the Boston Consulting Group (BCG) had developed and successfully marketed two management tools: 'The Experience Curve' (which suggested that those companies which had accumulated significant experience in the production of particular goods and services would reap the benefits of collapsing unit costs) and the 'Boston Matrix' (which offered the managers of conglomerate organisations a tool that, it was claimed, would measure market growth potential).

Within McKinsey there were fears that market developments of this sort were raising the reputation and profile of competitors at their expense. In an attempt to reverse this process, the senior management of McKinsey cast around for a tool, idea or technique that might serve to rebuild their reputation in the marketplace as leading-edge strategic thinkers.

In 1977, McKinsey launched three 'practices' on 'Strategy', 'Organisation' and 'Operations', respectively. These practices had a brief to consider the relationship between strategy, structure and effectiveness and to rejuvenate and rekindle the reputation of the firm. Tom Peters, who had recently returned to the company following a period of illness, was recruited to the 'Organisation Practice' and was dispatched on an eight-week trip to gather knowledge and information on the practices of 'effective organisations'. On the strength of this and other such knowledge gathering activities, the 'Organisation Practice' soon began to develop what was (for McKinsey and its clientele) a rather radical proposal. Thus the 'Organisation Practice' argued that focusing upon 'strategy' and 'structure' was unproductive in the absence of a more detailed appreciation of the organisational processes that put structures to work and strategies into action. Defining the problem in such negative terms was, of course, relatively easy for the 'Organisation Practice'. Stating a positive solution to the problem identified, however, proved to be more problematic.

In an attempt to bring some greater coherence to these stirrings concerning the limitations of what Peters is wont to dismiss as 'conventional' thinking on strategy and structure (see Peters and Waterman, 1982), McKinsey first paired Peters with a senior colleague – Bob Waterman – and then drafted in two academics – Anthony Athos, a pioneer in the field of corporate culture, and Richard Pascale.

While the precise mechanics of the process are disputed (see Crainer, 1997; Collins, 2007), all those involved tend to agree that, in time, this foursome (with the help of Julie Phillips, an associate from McKinsey) settled on seven words, beginning with the letter 's', designed to reflect their thinking as regards the organisational practices that allow businesses to develop and to act upon strategic plans. Thus the 'McKinsey 7-S model', which detailed a concern with 1) systems, 2) strategy, 3) structure, 4) style, 5) skills, 6) shared values and 7) staff, was born.

Early reaction to this model among McKinsey's partners and clientele was muted. Indeed, Crainer (1997) notes that between 1978 and 1979 Peters and his colleagues pitched their reflections on 'organisational effectiveness' to a number of potential clients but were unable to secure any business for the Organisation Practice. The organisations listening to Tom Peters' pitch were, it seems, amenable to the broad thrust of the analysis but doubted that this might be codified and applied to produce tangible business outcomes. Hewlett Packard, however, was persuaded and began to engage more fully with the project.[2] Furthermore, *Business Week* was sufficiently intrigued to publish a four-page article on the work of the Practice on July 21, 1980. In the 18 months following the publication of this short article, Peters gave 200 speeches, offered 50 workshops and secured a book deal which carried with it an advance (paltry by today's standards) of $5,000.

Peters, who was at this time increasingly unsettled within McKinsey, was granted a furlough to produce what would become *In Search of Excellence*. Thanks to Bob Waterman he was given a severance package which over five months paid the sum of $50,000. This cash was granted on the understanding that McKinsey would receive 50% of any royalties up to a maximum of 50,000 book sales. No one, however, actually anticipated that this figure would be reached. Indeed, the publishers expected the text to sell between 10,000 and 20,000 copies and so commissioned an initial print-run of 15,000.

Despite being free to focus his attention on the book, Tom Peters, it seems, struggled to produce a readable manuscript. In an attempt to put the project back on track, Bob Waterman was duly drawn in as co-author. Over time, and with patience on the part of the new co-author, Peters and Waterman together managed to develop a text which codified their instincts regarding business excellence. Thus Peters and Waterman argued that their excellent organisations exhibited eight common attributes. These attributes being:

1   A bias for action
2   Close to the customer
3   Autonomy and entrepreneurship
4   Productivity through people
5   Hands-on, value driven
6   Stick to the knitting
7   Simple form, lean staff
8   Loose-tight properties

This is, in a nutshell, the tale of how Peters and Waterman formed and articulated the core elements of what is now termed 'business excellence'. Yet to understand properly the appeal of the excellence project, we must move from a consideration of McKinsey's internal machinations to examine the factors in the wider socio-economic context, which made the core message of *In Search of Excellence* credible and persuasive.

The external context of excellence

Films produced in the US during the 1980s – even those which are framed as comedic – tend to portray an economy scarred by inequality and weighed down by a crumbling infrastructure. Due to limitations of space I will highlight but two examples: *Working Girl* and *Trading Places*. My apologies if I have ignored your favourite movie!

Working Girl is a romantic comedy starring Harrison Ford, Sigourney Weaver and Melanie Griffith. The tale centres upon Griffith's attempts to secure a career within New York's financial services sector. Griffith's character – Tess McGill – is doubly disadvantaged in this endeavour: She is female and (despite America's protestations to the contrary) working-class. Within this context Tess does not struggle to be noticed (she is routinely the subject of unwelcome sexual advances), but she does struggle to be taken seriously. In one particularly memorable scene, for example, Tess demands to be released from a limousine which has been rented by some overgrown frat boy in the hope of securing sexual favours. When Tess steps from the car, however, a fresh indignity awaits, and she is drenched by the displaced contents of a huge pothole which those charged with highway maintenance in the City of New York had failed to repair. In a similar fashion, *Trading Places*, a film featuring Eddie Murphy and Dan Aykroyd, offers a sustained (if comic) analysis of city trading and WASP prejudice. This film, like *Working Girl*, is set against the backdrop of a city which is obviously crumbling. Indeed, many of the key scenes feature derelict properties and vacant lots which suggest that the city, like the film's key characters, has been worn down by events. These and other contemporary Hollywood depictions (such as *Flashdance*) are, however, far from fantastical in their depictions of the US in this decade. Between 1981 and 1983, America endured a deep economic recession. Hyatt (1999) observes that, at this time, America had an unemployment rate in excess of 10%, an inflation rate approaching 15% and a banking interest rate in excess of 20%.

This set of economic circumstances was the worst America had suffered in five decades and led to street scenes which many thought (or hoped) had been consigned to an earlier period of history. *The Observer* (quoted in Baskerville and Willett, 1985), for example, reported that in Washington DC (the political hub of the US) 17,000 people had queued for up to five hours to receive food handouts. Similarly, the American Bureau of Census Statistics published figures which suggested that in 1983, 34.4 million Americans were living below the poverty line.

The feeling that something was rotten within the American economy (and within its structures of political governance) was reinforced by the impression that America, and Americans, were suffering while others (especially the Japanese) had manufactured an economic miracle. Fears regarding America's decline and the growing dominance of the Asian economies more generally had, of course, been troubling a number of commentators and many ordinary Americans before the recession of 1981–1983. As early as 1970, Kahn (1970) had predicted that Japanese *per capita* income would exceed the *per capita* income of the US by the year 2000. By 1978, however, Kahn (Kahn and Pepper, 1978) had revised his forecast and was now suggesting that Japan would be the new global economic superpower by 1980. This prediction proved to be wide of the mark, of course. Nonetheless the success of the Japanese economy in the post-war period was truly striking and did cause considerable anxiety in the US.

Pascale and Athos, early collaborators on the architecture of the excellence project (see Crainer, 1997; Collins, 2007), usefully document the success of Japan's economy and offer an explanation for this success:

> In 1980 Japan's GNP was third highest in the world and if we extrapolate current trends, it would be number one by the year 2000. A country the size of Montana, Japan has virtually no physical resources, yet it supports over 115 million people (half the population of the United States), exports $75 billion worth more goods than it imports, and has an investment rate as well as a GNP growth rate which is twice that of the United States. Japan has come to dominate in one selected industry after another – eclipsing the British in motorcycles, surpassing the Germans and Americans in automobile production, wresting leadership from the Germans and Americans and overcoming the United States' historical dominance in businesses as diverse as steel, shipbuilding, pianos, zippers and electronics . . . Japan is doing more than a little right. And our hypothesis is that a big part of that 'something' has only a little to do with such techniques as its quality circles and lifetime employment. In this book we will argue that a major reason for the superiority of the Japanese is their managerial skill.
>
> (Pascale and Athos, 1981: 20–21)

Expanding upon the nature of this 'managerial skill', Pascale and Athos argued that Japanese managers had successfully tapped into the emotions of their employees and in so doing had secured employee commitment to customers, to innovation and to change. Peters and Waterman accepted this analysis but were less willing to vaunt the skills of the Japanese. They argued that the disaster scenario outlined by Hayes and Abernathy (1980) could be averted if American managers could be persuaded a) of the need to re-balance the hard-S factors and the soft-S factors of business and b) to focus their energies on the eight attributes of business excellence identified through their research.

In Search of Excellence therefore conceded that Japanese managers had achieved something remarkable. Yet, despite the then often-voiced suggestion that Americans could choose either to work *like* the Japanese or *for* the Japanese (see Iacocca and Novak, 1984), *In Search of Excellence* insisted that there remained, within American management, practices that were worthy of emulation. Thus Peters and Waterman argued that rather than simply seeking to copy the practices of their Japanese counterparts, American managers could and should develop a form of executive leadership that would build upon the lessons available from America's best run companies.

Crainer (1997: 41) neatly captures the essential difference between those who suggested emulation of the Japanese and those who urged the renewal of a distinctly American approach. Thus he argues that the text developed by Pascale and Athos served 'humble pie' whereas *In Search of Excellence* offered 'apple pie'; an endorsement and celebration of America and its (espoused) values. It is worth pausing to consider the constituent components of this 'apple pie'.

A recipe for apple pie

Reflecting upon the developing economic crisis facing the US, *In Search of Excellence* argued that what had made America great in the 1940s and 1950s – its hard-S capabilities – had made it relatively weak in the 1970s. Consumer preferences, the authors argued, had altered to demand both quality and innovation (which Japan had delivered in spades!) but American business had simply failed to catch on. Rejecting the Taylorised separation of worker and managerial responsibilities, which characterised American manufacturing, Peters and Waterman argued that corporate leaders would need to develop cultures dedicated to customers, quality and innovation. Outlining the nature of the tools which would deliver such cultures, Peters and Waterman (1982) and later Peters and Austin (1985) argued that managers would need to seek out and should, where necessary, create opportunities to model the forms of thinking and action that would be needed to deliver quality and innovation for customers. Indeed Peters and his collaborators suggested that managers should – literally – take steps to establish themselves as a visible presence throughout the organisation; an approach that soon became known as MBWA, or management by wandering around. Highlighting the core purpose of MBWA, Peters and Waterman instructed practitioners to build and to share a web of stories designed to create models for thinking, feeling and acting in contexts otherwise dominated by division and ambiguity. Not all, however, found this rhetoric convincing.

Excellence: reception and backlash

Perhaps the most familiar and commonly voiced criticism raised against Tom Peters and what is now termed his 'excellence project' appeared in *Business Week* on November 5, 1984. Mocking Peters and Waterman, the cover of this periodical asked: 'Oops: Who's excellent now?'

Reviewing the track record of the excellent companies, this article observed that, just two years after the publication of *In Search of Excellence*, one third of the 'excellent' firms celebrated by Peters and Waterman were suffering some degree of financial distress!

We should not overlook the importance of this analysis and critique. It *is* well known and Tom Peters has repeatedly been challenged to offer a response. Yet this criticism is, actually, rather limiting as the basis for a critical review of *In Search of Excellence*. Indeed, this critique seems to accept the core elements of the excellence project – that there is a separate and distinctive category of excellent firms who stand proud of their peers – but mocks the authors for backing the wrong horses! Others, however, have looked longer and harder at the work of Peters and Waterman and have generated critical reviews on the excellence project, which question its outputs *and* the ideas, orientations and suppositions which constitute its inputs. One of the earliest of these critical reviews was produced by Carroll (1983), who offered an analysis of the methodological construction and the conceptual constitution of the excellence project.

In Search of Excellence argues that successful American firms have attributes in common which define them and which separate them from their less successful counterparts. Carroll counters, however, that Peters and Waterman built the excellence sample upon a methodology that is self-serving and upon a conceptualisation of business practice which sloppy, untested and indeed unverifiable. Highlighting the manner in which the excellence sample was developed, Carroll notes that Peters and Waterman formed their initial sample of firms simply by asking their McKinsey colleagues and other individuals connected to the world of business (such as journalists) to nominate those companies, which they regarded as being at the leading edge of practice. From this initial collection of firms the authors tell us that they proceeded to identify an initial group of 75 companies whose rating on six measures of financial performance made them leaders in their respective fields. From this grouping of 75 firms, Peters and Waterman tell us that they subsequently rejected 13 companies as failing to reflect the pattern of American business. Analysing the remaining 62 cases on a range of financial performance indicators (compound asset growth; compound equity growth; average ratio of market to book value; average return on total capital; average return on equity; average return on sales) Peters and Waterman decided that 18 of the remaining 62 companies were (probably) excellent but did not quite meet all of their criteria; a further 30 were agreed to be excellent according to the criteria, while a final grouping of 14 companies were said to represent exemplars of excellence. This graded sample we should note was developed by 'boosting' the scores awarded for innovation. Quite how this 'boosting' was organised is, however, left to the imagination of the reader!

Perhaps unsurprisingly, Carroll is dismissive of this approach to the calculation and codification of business excellence. He notes that the project begins with an *ad hoc* sample that reflects the orientations and predispositions of journalists and colleagues. Furthermore, he suggests that this initial and *ad hoc* sample becomes progressively corrupted as the authors allow their own biases and orientations to adjust the population in a self-serving and thoroughly unscientific manner. Elaborating on this theme, Guest (1992) notes that Peters and Waterman dismiss 13 members of their sample as flunking a test of 'representativeness' but fail to discuss the actual mechanics of this test. Guest notes that Peters and Waterman blithely 'boost' scores for innovation to benefit another 12 members of their sample, which on the basis of their own criteria, they had, previously excluded (see also Aupperle et al., 1986). Looking in more detail at the methodology of the excellence project, both Guest and Carroll complain that a great deal of weight is placed on anecdote and idiosyncratic recollection. Indeed, they observe that the data collected on the organisational practices of their 'excellent' organisations is undeserving of this grandiose and pseudo-scientific label for it is, too often, the outcome of a simple chat with a senior executive who would have obvious incentives to portray the organisation, and his (very few women appear in this book!) role within the organisation, in a positive light. Furthermore, Carroll (1983) observes that Peters and Waterman fail to study a less-than-excellent population. This oversight means that we cannot be sure that the attributes of excellence *are peculiar to, and characteristic of, excellent firms*. In this respect the excellence hypothesis is 'non-falsifiable' insofar as the methodology is constitutionally incapable of uncovering information that could refute the idea that excellent firms a) have attributes in common and that it is b) these eight attributes which denote and deliver business excellence. Highlighting the ramifications of this issue, Carroll (1983: 79) protests that the excellence project is flawed because it fails to recognise the ways in which factors such as 'proprietary technology, market dominance, control of critical raw materials, and national policy and culture' might have a bearing upon the fortunes of an organisation. He continues:

> Unfortunately, the most perfect adherence to the eight lessons [of excellence] will probably not permit 20 years of success against an IBM unless there is some sort of protective technology. Similarly oil companies without access to lower-cost oil supplies will suffer regardless of how well they implement the lessons [of *In Search of Excellence*].

Guest (1992) has also picked up on this theme. He observes that Peters and Waterman fail to discuss whether, in fact, all of the eight attributes of business excellence are actually necessary for stellar business success. Noting that a number of the attributes outlined do seem to overlap (for example attributes one, three and seven seem similar), Guest wonders if, say, six of the eight attributes of excellence constitute a sufficient basis for business success?

Van der Merwe and Pitt (2003) also question the extent to which firms would have to exhibit all eight of the attributes discussed by Peters and Waterman. However, the logic of the case put forward by van der Merwe and Pitt is different to that advanced by Guest. Firstly they observe that Peters and Waterman conjure a binary account of excellence. Like pregnancy, it seems, that you are either excellent or *not* excellent, there being no 'in-between' set of circumstances. Disputing the character of excellence (rather than the character of pregnancy), therefore, van der Merwe and Pitt suggest that business excellence might, more usefully, be construed as a continuum of possibilities.

Secondly van der Merwe and Pitt question the cultural appreciation of business at the heart of the excellence project. They argue that Peters and Waterman portray excellent organisations as culturally unified collectives. However, they counter that this simple-minded celebration of common purpose prevents us from acknowledging conflict within the collective, and so effectively precludes the meaningful analysis of organisational politics. Thirdly the authors invite us to consider the wider costs and benefits of the excellence project. They suggest that the excellence project will visit costs – technically known as 'externalities' – on other groups and constituencies who have been excluded from the analytical frame by Peters' and Waterman's celebration of organisational unity and common purpose.

Maidique (1983) offers a similar line of critique. She argues that the agreeable, if superficial, characteristics of this text (*it does contain good stories*) acts to obscure the fact that the argument is sloppily presented.

Crainer (1997) offers two concrete examples of such sloppiness. Firstly he notes that Peters and Waterman chose to exclude European firms from their narrative because these were said to be 'not fully representative of American business', yet the authors retained *Schlumberger* (a European firm) within their sample frame! Secondly Crainer observes that 15 of the companies applauded for their 'excellence' do not feature at all in the narrative developed by the authors while a further 42 members of this sample are mentioned fewer than five times.

Karl Weick (2004) chooses a different line of attack. He complains that *In Search of Excellence* is mistaken when it advocates a 'bias for action'. He argues that successful managers have 'a bias for talk'. As a comment on the nature of managerial work this is, of course, a perfectly sensible statement (see Collins, 2018). However, as a commentary on the work of Peters and Waterman, this statement could not be more wrong. Thus it is clear that in advocating what has become known as 'a bias for action', Peters and Waterman were, very clearly, telling managers that they would have to make real, personal and sustained efforts to *talk to* customers, colleagues and suppliers. Indeed, despite Weick's attack, the truth is that Peters and Waterman demonstrate, very clearly, their appreciation of the importance of talk and persuasion. Thus they suggest that in talking to customers, colleagues and suppliers, managers should work to create and to propagate stories that demonstrate the key attributes of excellence and their personal commitment to the quest. Despite Weick's attack, therefore, it is clear that the excellence project articulates clearly the understanding that managing is, at root, a social and (benignly) political process which depends upon talk, myth-making and storytelling for the prosecution of its ends.

In this regard, Watson's (2001) account of the legacy of the excellence project offers, I suggest, a more accurate, more balanced and ultimately a far more perceptive reading of the excellence project than all the other critiques raised against *In Search of Excellence*. While conceding that the excellence project is flawed conceptually and methodologically, therefore, Watson argues that *In Search of Excellence* remains a significant work because it offers a deeply human account of the processes of managing and organising. Contrasting this with Sloan's (Sloan et al., 1965) account of his time at the helm of General Motors, Crainer (1997) reminds us that this celebrated text is, in fact, bizarre because it contains, he tells us, no visible specimens of humanity.

Given the tendency to exclude or to diminish the presence 'the hewers of wood and the drawers of water', the excellence project succeeds, I suggest, and sets the pattern for all subsequent guru texts because it understands that managers, if they are to be successful, need to construct moral economies. In this regard and despite its manifest failings, the excellence project deserves to be taken seriously as the prototypical guru text. Yet to understand this developing market, we must pause to consider its fetters. In our next section, therefore, we will consider the changes necessary to bring the persuasive rhetoric of the excellence project to a mass audience.

Bringing management to the masses

Thus far we have considered the political and economic conditions prevailing in the US during the 1980s. We have suggested that fears of continuing economic decline and predictions of growing Japanese dominance prepared the way for representations of the business of management which diagnosed the cultural roots of the malaise while simultaneously advocating the pursuit of home-grown (and home-spun) remedies. This broad-brush account of the rise of management's gurus is plausible and generally accurate. But this narrative formulation is far from the whole truth for it fails to consider the changes within the fields of consulting, publishing and higher education, which were required to facilitate the popularisation of the managerial discourse that is guru theory. In this section we offer a very quick sketch of these changes.

Defining management

Engwall et al. (2016) observe that 'management' as we now understand the term, and as we now employ it to describe and to account for practices within a diverse range of settings, is a new form of expression. Yet they warn us that despite its novelty, the term 'management' is now so familiar to us that we are inclined to accept circular definitions of its nature and character. Such simplistic accounts of management are unhelpful, however, because they wrench the social-political practices of managing from the historical circumstances of its inception and development. In an attempt to understand the manner in which 'management', in effect, conquered the world, Engwall and his colleagues offer an historical analysis of business schools, management consultants and business publishing. Justifying their focus, the authors argue that these groupings warrant scrutiny because they have, in effect, defined our understanding of (good) 'management' through the construction and dissemination of a now dominant discourse that is embedded within taken-for-granted concepts such as 'best practice', 'world class performance' and, of course, 'business excellence'.

Management consultants

Kipping and Engwall (2003) suggest that the modern consulting firms which shape our lives evolved from the 'time and motion' specialists who emerged in the early years of the twentieth century. McKenna (2007), however, disputes this. The modern management consultancies, he suggests, were quite unlike their forebears and were in fact very careful to signal the manner in which their conduct and ethics were similar to those prevailing in the more respected legal practices. Both sides of this debate, however, do seem to agree that management consultants had to make serious efforts to establish themselves as legitimate authorities on matters of business and administration.

Commenting upon the development of McKinsey and Co, Edersheim (2004) observes that Marvin Bower, a lawyer by training, worked very carefully to model his developing consulting firm upon the conduct which prevailed within the most prestigious law firms and took steps to enforce standards of behaviour and dress among his associates. Behavioural and institutional changes such as these, Engwall et al. (2016) suggest, enabled the leading consulting firms to emerge as apostles of 'management'. Paradoxically, however, the factors which had allowed the consulting firms to define and to advance 'management' acted, initially, as impediments to the articulation and dissemination of 'popular management'.

Reflecting upon the genesis of the excellence project, Collins (2007) notes that Tom Peters had to overcome internal opposition within McKinsey and Co simply to be allowed to write a book on managerial matters. Indeed, Collins observes that Peters was, in fact, obliged by his employers to change the title of his now famous text. Thus it appears that that Tom Peters had originally intended to suggest that his book would provide *the secrets of excellence* but was warned off by his employers. McKinsey, which had established itself as a beacon for 'best practice' *within* the arena of consulting, argued that the title proposed by Peters was unacceptable on two counts. Firstly the title suggested that McKinsey might be inclined to betray client privilege. Secondly the title suggested that the firm was simply prepared to surrender proprietary knowledge that might otherwise be monetised. Given this posture it is, perhaps, unsurprising that between 1960 and 1980 McKinsey agreed to the publication of just two books by its staff, neither of which could be considered to be inviting prospects. In the early 1980s, however, all this changed. Emboldened by the success of *In Search of Excellence*, staff members working for McKinsey produced no fewer than 50 texts, many of which secured a global market presence for the authors and for McKinsey (see Crainer, 1997). We now turn to consider the publishers of 'popular management' texts.

Publishers

The publishers who deliver popular management may well be drawn to the companies they serve by a love of books or through some yearning to pen their own works of art, but these individuals work within a commercial context which in recent decades has been marked by takeover and conglomeration (Engwall et al., 2016). Acknowledging the commercial pressures which shape publishing and which encourage a search for 'the next big thing', Clark (2004) highlights the manner in which editors (among others) constitute a fashion-setting community dedicated to spotting, nurturing and/or creating new trends. Indeed, Clark (2004) suggests that editors and the associated members of the publishing industry's fashion-setting community (such as those who must sell advertising space within journals) have a vested interest in identifying and promoting new trends with which organisations are then obliged to engage. A key component of the publishing industry that services 'popular management' is, of course, the ghost-writers, editors and researchers who, as McKenna (2016) shows, have done much to craft our understanding of 'good management' and its core problematics. We will now turn to consider these problematics as we consider those engaged in 'research' on management.

Higher education

Engwall and his colleagues (2016) observe that business education struggled to gain a legitimate position within seats of higher learning and had to overcome prejudices associated with the provision of 'training' (as opposed to education) and the pursuit of 'trade'. Discussing the American context, they suggest that the developing business schools attempted to overcome such prejudice by forging linkages with the established and accepted schools (like 'law'), which derived their authority from ideals of professionalism. In other contexts – Germany, for example – legitimacy was, they suggest, developed and secured through a public commitment to the scientific method.

Commenting upon the manner in which the field of business education facilitates and is drawn into 'popular management', Clark (2004) suggests that business schools in the US (and to a lesser extent the UK) are now active participants in 'popular management' in at least two ways. Firstly the employees of business schools (especially in the US), he argues, pen popular management texts and through their teaching induct neophytes into the problematics of mainstream management. Secondly the educational process endured by students prepares graduates to accept and to seek new solutions and, in so doing, builds future markets for the wares of the consulting industry. Highlighting the manner in which business schools have challenged (and traduced) the principles and ethos of higher education (see Kuhrana, 2007), Brindle and Stearns (2001) argue that the leading advocate of 'good management', the *Harvard Business Review*, has effectively abandoned any pretence to academic rigour to become, instead, a high-profile enabler of the representations of work, management and competition which are now central to guru theorising.

This, in the form of a thumb-nail sketch, offers some indication of the demand-pull conditions and supply-side changes necessary to propagate the multi-billion dollar industry that is 'popular management'. Yet our sketch has, thus far, failed to offer any real consideration of the consumers of guru theory. In our next section we will consider these users who are, as we shall see, often dismissed as being just too dim to recognise that they are ill-served by the gurus of management.

Five waves of fashion

Grint (1997a, 1997b) offers five overlapping explanations for the waves of management fashion that have crashed over both practitioners and the academy since the 1980s. Grint's position on these fashion waves is, publicly at least, 'agnostic' (see chapter four). He is therefore concerned to examine the different ways in which we might account for and, in so doing, come to terms with the fashions which now construct and shape management. In this he offers an opportunity to develop a balanced appreciation of guru theory *and* an opportunity to preface ideas on rhetoric which we will pursue in chapter four.

Grint's first explanation for the waves of managerial fashion offers the simplest and most clearly rationalist approach. Channelling the rhetorical sensibilities of the gurus (who insist that a combination of changing tastes, wpetition which will crush organisational laggards), Grint argues that one way to explain management fashions would be to accept that in such times of change they constitute a persuasive rhetoric which actually engineers useful market and behavioural outcomes. Grint's first and simplest explanation for the successive waves of management fashion, therefore, is based upon the suggestion that managers act rationally when they select guru theory because these representations allow organisations to select innovations that will keep them ahead of competitors in a fast-changing environment. What others would dismiss as empty, fashionable ideas constituted upon faddish notions therefore might be said to constitute an 'efficient-choice' (Abrahamson, 1991, 1996) during times of change.

Grint's second explanation for the waves of change in management suggests that managerial thought/practice comes in waves. Observing that managerial waves alternate between the 'soft' approach advocated by Peters and Waterman (1982) and the 'hard' approach preferred by Taylor (1911) and more recently Hammer (1990), Grint argues that it is possible to map changes in managerial ideology against Kondratieff's (1935) long waves of economic and technological development. Building upon the work of Barley and Kunda (1992), Grint suggests that Kondratieff cycles are matched by similar swings in management ideology. Thus the expansion phase of a

Kondratieff wave seems to promote a rationalist ideology, while the decline of any particular Kondratieff wave, he suggests, seems more closely associated with normatively based approaches to management. Grint's second explanation, which might be termed a 'structural requirements' explanation, therefore, suggests once again that managers act rationally in their pursuit of fashion. Thus the structural requirements explanation suggests that those managers who properly identify the managerial ideology appropriate to the phase of economic development steal an advantage over rivals who fail to innovate. In this respect the structural requirements explanation adds context and chronology to the business concerns which underpin explanation one, insofar as it suggests that 'rational' managers will change their approach in an attempt to tailor the form and style of management to the phase of economic development.

Grint's third explanation for the succession of managerial waves focuses upon the inadequacies (real or otherwise) of the leaders of organisations. Noting that it is the senior members of organisations who choose to implement new waves in management, Grint argues that we should attempt to understand those factors which influence and impact upon the sense-making and choice-making activity of senior managers. Thus Grint argues that we must, when discussing the take-up of fashionable ideas, acknowledge the extent to which guru theory gurus encourage senior managers to respond emotionally, politically and so selfishly to managerial innovations. As Grint notes:

> one should note the significance of being regarded as a fashion-setter rather than a fashion-taker. If part of the attraction of the consultant as charismatic is that some of the charisma may rub off on those who are first to use the latest technique then we might explain the desire of CEOs to throw themselves on to the experimental altar.
>
> (Grint, 1997b: 733)

Grint's fourth wave is informed by a reading of Veblen (1994). Veblen argues that material abundance has acted to blur status divisions in society. Given this, Veblen argues that high status groupings will tend to seek new products and new experiences as they attempt to distance themselves from lower status groups. For example, wealthy and fashion conscious consumers patronise 'exclusive' forms of design and 'exclusive' holiday destinations. However, should these labels and resorts become affordable to the masses, the higher status grouping will quickly define them as passé and will move on to other, still 'exclusive' forms of consumption, in order to distance themselves from the *hoi polloi*.

Grint argues that this general tactic of social distancing might help to explain the willingness of managers to embrace new fashions. Thus Grint suggests that managers may choose to adopt new ideas in order to mark themselves out as special, distinctive, better than the rest. Grint's fourth explanation for the attractions of guru theorising, therefore, 'has less to do with the performance of the consultant or the logical promise of radical business improvements and more to do with the emotional significance of internal status and identity construction in the face of increasing complexity' (Grint, 1997b: 735).

The fifth argument deployed to explain the waves of management fashion, again, acknowledges that managers are subject to normative pressures at work. These pressures, Grint suggests, make it necessary to demonstrate that you, as a practitioner of management, are not *just* a manager but a leader; a visionary at the head of affairs. To be a leader, Grint suggests, one must be at the cutting edge of ideas. Given this pressure, Grint suggests that the truly aspirant manager cannot risk being viewed as being out-of-date or out-of-step and, as a result, feels pressure to embrace each new wave of fashion. Thus Grint suggests that, far from being the hapless victims of a fashion-setting industry, managers may choose to patronise innovations even when they suspect these to be flawed, because there are status and career benefits associated with being at the head of the pack. In this regard Grint's analysis moves us from a unitary account (Fox, 1985) of common goals (explawna-tions one and two) to accept the existence of a rational calculus underpinning the pursuit of fashion. Grint's analysis invites us to acknowledge local adaptation shaped by organisational pluralism. This, we would do well to note, is a form of pluralism which, while explicable, is not necessarily laudable and a very long way from the salvation of *our* corporations advocated for example by Hilmer and Donaldson (1996). Thus Grint's final explanation for popular management suggests that guru theory is problematic because in serving the interests of an organisational elite it will tend to generate significant externalities for others within and beyond the organisation.

Concluding comments

This chapter has offered an analysis of the rise of management's gurus. It has argued that management's gurus are very much products of the 1980s and need to be located within this socio-historical context.

The standard narrative used to explain the rise of management's gurus tends to suggest that the representations which underpin guru theory need to be understood as products of the political and economic crisis that gripped America in the early 1980s. This explanation is not categorically 'wrong', but it is far from being the 'whole story' since it fails to concede that, despite the crisis, the rise of *the* gurus was, in truth, unexpected and pretty unlikely. In an attempt to account for this surprising turn of events we have examined the genesis of the excellence project. We have argued that *In Search of Excellence* needs to be understood as a 'game-changer' whose success enabled a shift in the posture of the consulting firms who were dominant in this period. Building upon the analysis of Engwall et al. (2016), however, we have argued that the consulting firms are but one fork on the trident that has delivered guru theory to the masses. Recognising this, we have highlighted the ways in which shifts within the fields of education and business publishing acted to build and to secure a mass-market for the representations of business and management which underpin guru theory. Finally, we concluded with brief reflections on the manner in which guru theory is received and consumed by its users.

In our next chapter we will consider a range of analytical responses to guru theorising as we analyse what Collins (2000) has termed the 'guru industry'.

Notes

1 The gurus of management are, of course, predominantly male.
2 There appears to be some confusion here: Siemens (see Collins, 2007) is sometimes listed as the pioneering organisation that had the vision to embrace the excellence project.

4   The 'guru industry'

Introduction

In this chapter we develop our critical understanding of the ways and means of guru theorising through an analysis of what I have (elsewhere) dubbed the 'guru industry' (Collins, 2000). I first introduced this concept in a book produced some 20 years ago and have since that time returned periodically to the concept to offer minor refinements. These refinements have been developed, largely, to offer a more economical analysis and presentation (see for example Collins, 2003, 2015, 2019). In this chapter I offer a more thorough review and reanalysis of the 'guru industry'. The updated analysis developed here offers a critical re-statement of the 'guru industry' which, as we shall see, is quite unlike those previously produced. That said the re-statement of the 'guru industry' outlined here has, like its forerunners, been designed to provide a means to analyse and to classify (key) commentaries that have grown up around gurus and guru theorising.

In previous chapters we observed that the gurus of management might be said to be a component of an industry dedicated to the production of representations of work and management which are a) positive and b) focused upon securing change within organisations and across civic life more generally. In addition, we observed that in pursuit of this endeavour, the gurus have combined with researchers, publishers, ghost-writers and party-planners, to name only a few of the key nodes within this network. In this chapter we will use the term 'guru industry' in a more restricted and specialised sense.

In this chapter the term 'guru industry' will be used to refer to a group of writers and commentators who live in the shadow (or in the reflected glory) of the gurus and who have drafted works which in a variety of ways comment upon, or offer distillations of, the ideas of the gurus of management. Those active in the 'guru industry' then are not themselves gurus, although some of those active in this arena may earn a proportion of their income as 'researchers', 'ghost-writers' and 'consulting editors'.[1] Equally, while some members of this 'guru industry' may move in social orbits which overlap with those populated by the gurus, the members of our 'guru industry' tend to move professionally at lower levels of valence.

In earlier renderings of this 'guru industry' I suggested that this collective might be considered to be analogous to the 'Braverman Industry', which Eldridge (1983) observed had grown up around Braverman's (1974) *Labor and Monopoly Capital*. Commenting upon this Braverman Industry, Eldridge suggested that while it had improved our appreciation of Taylorism, many of the commentaries published on *Labor and Monopoly Capital* were overly-critical and failed to acknowledge some of Braverman's more nuanced insights. As we shall see, the guru industry also includes commentaries that some might consider to be unnecessarily critical of the gurus. Yet we must also acknowledge that the 'guru industry', quite unlike the Braverman Industry, also includes reflections on the gurus of management that are, by any standards, simplistic and uncritical. In addition, we should acknowledge that the writings offered by those working within the 'guru industry' are rather more varied and altogether more diverse than guru theory itself. This outcome arises, I suggest, because there is, within the guru industry, no common 'idea family' such as that observed by Huczynski (1993). Furthermore, we must concede that no account of the 'guru industry' could ever hope to be exhaustive or encyclopaedic. Given this and given our earlier comments concerning the perils of *listeria*, this chapter does not pretend to offer an exhaustive bibliography of the 'guru industry'. Instead, the chapter offers a framework designed to allow readers to locate, to understand and to critique the different ways in which commentators have sought to come to terms with the gurus and their preferred representations of managing and organising.

Accordingly, our chapter is structured is follows: We begin with an overview of the 'guru industry'. The second section will sketch the continuum developed to explain and to account for this loose collective. Having secured an appreciation of this continuum, the third section will offer an account of those contributions to the 'guru industry' that might be said to be hagiologic in character. The fourth, fifth and sixth sections of this chapter will offer analyses of the remaining components of the 'guru industry' and, in common with the third section, will consider the manner in which theory and practice are constituted within those domains concerned with 'redemptive texts', 'agnostic' analyses, and 'atheistic' rebuttals of guru theorising. We will then conclude with a brief summary of the chapter.

A framework for analysis

Discussing the similarities between guru theory and (Christian) theology, Pattison (1997) observes that the world of the gurus is not simply secular but often plainly godless. Nonetheless, he argues that the term 'guru' has utility in the field of management. Explaining his rationale, Pattison argues that the term guru is fitting in this secular context because, like the religious prophet, the guru 'conjures up a dualistic, polarized world' (Pattison, 1997: 139). Where the religious prophet offers a vision of a world polarised between good and evil, heaven and hell, salvation and damnation, the management guru, Pattison tells us, 'conjures up a dualistic, polarised world in which businesses are either conspicuously successful or conspicuous flops' (139). Yet guru accounts of the business world cannot begin and end with description. To qualify as a guru, prescription must be coupled to description. In common with the religious prophet, therefore, the management guru offers 'easy-to-grasp principles of salvation' (Pattison, 1997: 135) which disciples may use to (re)structure their lives.

Discussing Tom Peters' *Thriving on Chaos* (1988), Pattison argues that, in this work, Peters 'clearly reveals his charismatic, prophetic nature' (Pattison, 1997: 135). Indeed, Pattison insists that *Thriving on Chaos* is 'a work full of religious style, insights and language' (135). Echoing Latour's (1987) account of the manner in which those who would build new worlds in our name establish the efficacy of their concerns, Pattison suggests that *Thriving on Chaos* has been designed to build upon a familiar biblical tale and, in being constituted in these terms, moves us quickly 'downstream' to a position where earlier assertions and conjectures are accepted as being substantial and plainly uncontroversial. To illustrate this point (and our hydraulic metaphor), we offer a cascading account of the core narrative of *Thriving on Chaos*. As we shall see, this cascade moves us quickly *from* fear and conjecture *to* salvation and certainty. Thus the core message of *Thriving on Chaos* may be rendered as follows:

1   The 'promised land' is under threat. Fierce competition from foreign shores threatens the 'good life' enjoyed by Americans.
2   This foreign challenge has arisen because those in charge of American industry have failed to realise that the 'old order' is passing away. This old order was built upon rationalist planning. However the emergent 'new order' resists rationalism. The future, therefore, can no longer be mapped, or planned for, by extrapolating from the past.
3   Salvation is at hand. But to see this promised land, recognition of the chaotic nature of our organised existence must be embraced.
4   Individuals and organisations will need to earn the right of entry to the promised land. They must turn their back upon coldly rationalistic approaches to management in order to meet the challenges which 'chaos' brings.
5   It would be folly to delay! Tomorrow it may be too late to change.
6   Rewards await those who embrace chaos and who are prepared to master its managerial challenges.

Höpfl's (2005) analysis of contemporary organising practices confirms Pattison's (1997) reading of the rhetoric of guru theorising. Yet Höpfl questions the virtues of the salvation on offer.

Reflecting upon Christian theology, Höpfl (2005: 172) notes that 'there are two related notions which are attendant on Judgement: the bad are cast into darkness, into a place where they can no longer see and which, itself, is unseen. The good enter Heaven where they can see clearly for the first time'. Conversely, Höpfl notes that those refused entry to the Kingdom of Heaven endure the punishment of loss (*poena damni*) and the punishment of the senses (*poena sensus*).

Offering a critical reappraisal of the salvation promised by the gurus of management, Höpfl (2005: 174) observes that the secularised theology of the gurus represents 'an extraordinary inversion of the tents of Christian theology' because the salvation attendant upon devotion to the gurus requires conformity to a system of working that diminishes the individual within the organisational collective. This system, she warns us will cause both a loss of self and a punishment of the senses. Indeed, Höpfl (2005: 174) argues that 'the *poena damni*; the punishment of loss', is a condition of entry to the contemporary work organisation. It is, she tells us, 'precisely the physical, the good, the worthy, the social justice and the dignity of the individual which has to be abandoned as a condition of entry' to those organisations shaped by the family of ideas that is guru theory.

Noting that the individual entering the excellent workplace also confronts the punishment of the senses, Höpfl argues that the *poena sensus* is 'obvious in the demands of work as long hours, physical and/or mental labour' (174) consequent upon a commitment to the customer and to the practices of business excellence. These demands, she warns, lead to 'anguish, stress and ill health' (174).

Recognising the importance of religious allusion within the works of the gurus, the framework for the 'guru industry' outlined here self-consciously employs religious imagery. The continuum which describes this framework (see Figure 4.1) therefore divides the 'guru industry' into four key groupings.[2] Moving from left to right, these groupings represent:

- Hagiologies
- Redemptive texts
- Agnostic texts
- Atheistic readings of the guru industry

Readers who would prefer a slightly more secularised rendering of the gurus may take heart from the fact that the 'guru industry' might also be considered to be a continuum of three plausible responses to the gurus of management. These responses might be said to range *from* hagiology *through* apology *to* apoplexy (see Collins, 2003 and Figure 4.2).

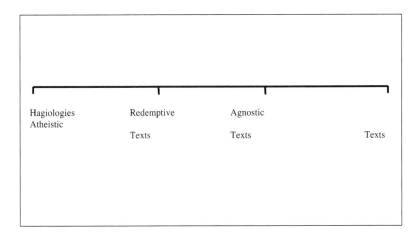

Figure 4.1 The 'guru industry'

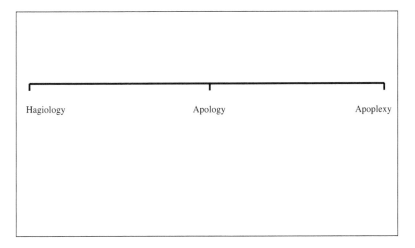

Figure 4.2 An alternative rendering of the 'guru industry'

Hagiologies

Many commentaries on the gurus of management adopt a highly deferential approach to the subjects of their analyses. Indeed a number of texts which feature in the 'guru industry' seem to be designed as devotions to the gurus. In these devotional texts, the gurus of management are plainly regarded as special. The gurus are, it is clear, to be regarded as visionaries who are worthy of our veneration. Texts exhibiting such features, I suggest, deserve to be termed 'hagiologies'. To illustrate the nature and character of such hagiological texts, I will offer a brief reprise (see chapter two) of Kennedy's ([1991] 1996) text and Crainer's (1998a) self-styled *Ultimate Guide*.

Kennedy's *Managing with the Gurus* ([1991] 1996) aims to offer, as its sub-title suggests, 'top level guidance on 20 management techniques'. It attempts to supply this 'top level guidance' by distilling from the works of the gurus the key ideas which Kennedy believes 'top' managers require in order to remain successful. The unspoken argument of Kennedy's book, therefore, is really quite simple and goes something like this: A number of thinkers and scholars have written a great deal about management which you as a 'top manager' should be able to repeat in meetings, at conference events and during selection interviews. The problem being, of course, that as a 'top manager' you are simply too busy to read about that which you insist you already perform at the very highest levels of capability. To free you from this burden, Kennedy has taken this task upon herself. She has therefore read the key texts which 'top managers' should know (but don't), and having read these works, has selected the important passages which, she insists, 'continue to resonate' (Kennedy, [1991] 1996: 1). These extracts, she tells us, should be considered to be 'torch-beams' (2). They are therefore worthy of reproduction and public exhibition because they retain the capacity to 'inspire and aid people struggling with the disciplines of management' (2).

Kennedy's text is structured as follows. After a brief preface, she spends a few moments detailing the lives of the 43 gurus she has highlighted as being worthy of celebration. We are told their dates of birth (and, where appropriate, the date of death), and we are offered a small biography, which spells out the notable achievements and accomplishments of each guru. Following this, Kennedy takes us on a tour of 20 chapters where, following brief introductory remarks, extracts from the works of these 43 gurus are reproduced, in order to provide illumination and inspiration on topics such as 'the craft of management', 'culture', 'motivation', 'quality' and 're-engineering'.

This book I have labelled 'a hagiology' because in its tone and mode of presentation it is much like those edifying texts which the Christian church (in a variety of denominational guises) has produced as celebrations of its saints (see Baring-Gould, 1914).

Yet Kennedy's educational ambition is marred by a number of unhelpful presumptions. Firstly she too readily assumes that we can easily form a consensus as to the membership of the elite cadre of commentators taken to represent *the* gurus. Secondly Kennedy's work grants to *the* gurus the only voice in the process of managerial decision-making. Accordingly, her account of the wit and wisdom of *the* gurus fails either to recognise or to account for organisational plurality, and so fails meaningfully to account for the possibility of some dispute as to the means and ends of organisa-tions. Thirdly we should note that, in the absence of a meaningful account of organisational politics, Kennedy is obliged to fall back on a very naïve model of management which assumes that otherwise sensible individuals will respond to the stated 'needs' of the organisation in an altruistic fashion. Fourthly Kennedy's work appears to assume that management thought and practice proceeds in a linear fashion, with outdated ideas being driven out by novel innovations. Grint's (1994) analysis, however, suggests that suc-cessful guru ideas notable for their conservatism and for their familiarity.

Yet in all this, Kennedy is not alone. Crainer's (1998a) *Ultimate Guide* offers a similarly hagiologic account of the gurus of management and exhibits similar problems. That said, we should acknowledge that unlike Kennedy, Crainer does not pretend to offer a definitive listing of management's gurus (although this does seem to render his title meaningless). Furthermore Crainer, at least initially, appears to express some degree of scepticism regarding the gurus and their works. Pondering the phenomenal growth of the gurus, he notes:

> The sheer mass of new material suggests that quantity comes before quality. *There is a steady supply of new insights into old ideas.* Manage-ment theorizing has become adept at finding new angles on old topics.
> (Crainer, 1998a: xiv, emphasis added)

In the main body of the text, however, it soon becomes apparent that Crain-er's attitude to the gurus is, like Kennedy's, largely hagiologic in charac-ter. Thus while Crainer's account eschews hagiography, his overall tone is clearly similar to that voiced by Kennedy. In spite of his initial scepticism, therefore, Crainer is, in fact, rather devoted to his gurus. Indeed, we would do well to note that the dust-jacket of my copy protests that the best and most successful companies enjoy commercial prosperity because they have followed the advice proffered by the gurus. Guest's (1992) analysis of busi-ness excellence, however, contradicts Crainer's assertion. Thus Guest sug-gests that the successful companies of the early 1980s enjoyed good results precisely because they had avoided the advice that had been made available to business organisations in the 1970s.

The brief overview of the hagiologies developed here, in concert with the analysis of personification offered in chapter two, demonstrates that the hagiologists of the 'guru industry' have produced laudatory accounts of *the* gurus. Unfortunately, these catalogues proceed in the absence of any meaningful reflection on the nature of management. In addition, they fail to reflect critically on the nature and development of management knowledge. Furthermore, they are marred by inconsistencies which arise due to what my teenage children would refer to as 'flexing'.

Flexing

At root, the concept of 'flexing' alludes to the contraction of the visible musculature – primarily biceps – which occurs (especially) when teenage boys, taken by notions of masculinity, seek to establish their strength/attractiveness before their peers. Used more metaphorically, 'flexing' denotes circumstances where an individual within a social context seeks either to secure an advantage or to establish superiority over their contemporaries. 'Name-dropping' (suggesting friendship/familiarity with a high-profile individual), for example, might be taken to be a form of 'flexing' within this more metaphorical setting.

The hagiologists of the 'guru industry', I suggest, also tend to engage in 'flexing' when compiling their guru listings. Thus the hagiologists seem unable to resist adding the names of philosophers and sociologists, partly read and dimly remembered from college days, to their catalogues. The inclusion of these sociologists and philosophers within published listings of the gurus does bring a veneer of academic respectability to what is, otherwise, just a collection of rich Americans, minor celebrities and DWEMs.[3] Yet pressing these individuals into service adds little to what is an intellectually dubious endeavour. Thus the philosophers and sociologists exhibited within these hagiologies appear in a very much reduced form. Indeed, their works are traduced by an over-arching manifesto which is narrowly instrumental and chauvinistic.

Redemptive texts

Management's gurus, as we have seen, claim to offer salvation to those struggling to deal with the challenges thrown up by a volatile competitive context. The hagiologists of the 'guru industry' welcome this intervention and have chosen to produce texts that celebrate the wit and wisdom of *the* gurus. Those texts which I have styled as redemptionist in character choose a different path. Unlike the hagiologists, therefore, the redemptionists suggest that we should put our faith in managers and must now intervene to save management from the clutches of the gurus. This is, at one level, a very laudable goal. The problem, as we shall see, however, is that these avowedly redemptionist texts tend to develop analyses which are both anti-guru *and* anti-manager.

In an attempt to elaborate, I will offer a brief analysis of what I take to be three significant and widely available redemptive texts. These are the works produced by Hilmer and Donaldson (1996), Micklethwait and Wooldridge (1997) and Brindle and Stearns (2001).

Management's redeemers

Hilmer and Donaldson (1996: xi) protest that the prominent position which the gurus enjoy in public life signals 'the substitution of dogma – platitudes, homilies and fads – for careful, sustained professional management'. In an attempt to redeem management from these gurus, Hilmer and Donaldson argue that those who shoulder managerial responsibility should reject the fads of management and should instead develop/deploy their *own* analytical skills. Thus Hilmer and Donaldson suggest:

• that the gurus of management disrupt and damage organisations because they focus upon technique and so belittle the skills, talents and training of those who have worked hard to appreciate the dilemmas that characterise managerial work; and
• that the texts prepared by the hagiologists amount to 'bluffers' guides' for dilettantes who fail to conduct themselves professionally.

There is, however, a rather significant problem with the line of argument developed by Hilmer and Donaldson. The authors never actually qualify the term that is central to their argument; that is to say that they fail to define 'management fad'. The authors do, of course, protest that fads have panacea-like qualities insofar as they represent cure-all remedies (see Collins, 2012a, 2015). Furthermore, the authors suggest that (so-called) fads diminish the essential challenges that arise in connection with the animation and orientation of others. Yet, it is plain that in the work of Hilmer and Donaldson, the term 'fad' is a term of abuse masquerading as an analytical category.

In an attempt to overcome the easy disparagement which is enabled by the casual application of the fad motif, Abrahamson (1991, 1996) develops a neo-institutional form of analysis which understands that organisations are obliged to respond purposefully to a variety of laws, regulations and expectations. Recognising this, he invites us to think of 'fads' in an analytical, non-pejorative manner.

Abrahamson does seem to struggle to use the term 'fad' in a qualified sense. At times he uses the term as a simple synonym for fashion:

Modes, vogues, fads, fashions, rages and crazes frequently revolutionize many aspects of cultural life.

(Abrahamson, 1996: 254)

Yet at other times, he uses these terms quite separately. Indeed, in an earlier paper, Abrahamson (1991) suggests that we should separate 'management fashions' from 'management fads'. His insistence that such innovations need to be considered from the standpoint of rhetoric, however, remains constant throughout. Thus Abrahamson (1996: 254) defines fashions and fads as 'transitory collective beliefs that certain management techniques are at the forefront of management projects'.

Abrahamson complains that scholars of management have failed to take fashion seriously and have, indeed, tended to treat fashion as being trivial and undeserving of serious scholarly intention. Disputing this orientation, he suggests that management fashion is worthy of serious scrutiny and yet quite unlike 'aesthetic fashion'. Aesthetic fashion, Abrahamson argues, is a social-psychological phenomenon that makes an appeal to *taste* and *beauty* whereas the rhetoric (and appeal) of management fashion is couched in terms of *rationality* and *progress*. To explore this rhetorical formulation, he considers four explanations for recent developments in management knowledge (see Figure 4.3).

Abrahamson labels the first of his four explanations for management fashion 'Efficient Choice'. In this quadrant it is assumed that organisational actors can a) interpret market signals accurately and can b) develop innovations designed to respond to these signals. Abrahamson plainly doubts the efficacy of this rationalistic account of managing. Nonetheless, he allows it as a possibility (albeit an implausible one). Thus he suggests that in this quadrant organisational innovations represent rational and progressive attempts to reduce the gap between actual and potential performance.

The second perspective Abrahamson labels 'Forced Selection'. In common with the first perspective, this quadrant assumes that organisational actors face little in the way of uncertainty. In this sector of the diagram, therefore, it is clear what actors need to do in any given situation. Yet here the conduct of actors is less volitional than in the first perspective. Indeed, discretion is assumed to be constrained by external agencies that have the power to mandate certain courses of action and/or organisational forms.

The third quadrant Abrahamson labels the 'Fashion' perspective. Here, 'fashion' is not synonymous with 'fad'. Indeed, 'fads' are analysed in the fourth quadrant and are said to reflect a different dynamic.

	Imitation processes do not impel diffusion or rejection of ideas	Imitation processes impel the diffusion or rejection of ideas
Orgainzations within a group determine the diffusion and rejection of ideas within the group	Efficient-Choice Perspective	Fad Perspective
Organizations outside a group determine the diffusion and rejection within the group	Forced-Selection Perspective	Fashion Perspective

Figure 4.3 Abrahamson's (1991) analysis of the diffusion and rejection of managerial ideas

Within this fashion perspective, organisational actors are said to confront a complex environment such that there is uncertainty about a) the goals of the organisation and b) the efficiency of organisational innovations. These uncertainties are said to generate fear and anxiety among organisational actors. In an attempt to allay these anxieties, practitioners are said to turn to 'fashion-setters', or consultants, for support and guidance.

Commenting upon the mechanics of this argument, Thomas (1999) notes three models of the fashion-setting process:

1 The 'trickle-down' model, where high status groups act as models, or exemplars, which other lower status, but aspirant, groups will tend to emulate.
2 'Collective selection theory', which assumes that collective movements in fashion and taste allows individuals to satisfy their felt need for change from within the relative safety of the group.
3 The 'marionette model', which assumes that fashion swings are the inevitable outcome of capitalist social relations because we are socialised a) to think of ourselves as consumers and b) to demand novelty.

Viewed in the context of these accounts of the fashion-setting process, it is apparent that Abrahamson's third quadrant operates, largely, with a 'trickle-down' model of fashion since here we have organisational isomorphism in the absence of coercion. Abrahamson's 'Fad' perspective, in contrast, appears to employ a model of 'collective selection theory'. In this, the fourth quadrant outlined by Abrahamson (1991), organisational actors are assumed to be uncertain about their goals *and* about the efficiency of organisational innovations. Yet, in the absence of a fashion-setting community, those located within this quadrant are obliged to find a means of dealing with their own anxieties. In this sector of the diagram, the actual outcome is much like that hypothesised for the fashion perspective. Thus the organisations in this arena begin to look alike and to do the same things. Yet the mechanics of this isomorphism differ.

In the fashion perspective, isomorphism is the result of the activities of a fashion-setting community selling innovations. In the fad perspective, however, organisational isomorphism is a product of mimesis. Thus, in the absence of a fashion-setting community, actors in similar market/organisational niches are said to manage their own anxieties and the expectations of wider stakeholders (Abrahamson, 1996) by adopting similar tools, forms and/or innovations.

In Abrahamson's (1991) schema, quadrants one and two are pro-innovation. These quadrants assume that management is rational and that choices with respect to innovation reflect a choice-making process that is, similarly, rational and transparent. Hilmer and Donaldson (1996) accept one half of this. Management, they aver, is amenable to rational choice-making. However, these authors insist that the tools and pre-dispositions of the consulting industry encourage managers to behave irrationally.

In quadrants three and four, Abrahamson addresses this division between the rational and the irrational and in so doing he questions the casual unitarism that characterises much of the literature on fads and fashions. Thus Abrahamson argues that certain forms of conduct which might appear to be irrational to academic eyes are perfectly rational when (re)placed within the context of their application. Thus Abrahamson suggests that managers are obliged to embrace 'norms of progress'. Under conditions of uncertainty and in circumstances where stakeholders expect managers to be both proactive and at the forefront of innovation, Abrahamson argues that it is perfectly rational to place your faith in fashion-setters – even when you harbour suspicions as to the utility of their products – because this is the form of conduct that organisations and market-makers reward.

Abrahamson's analytical separation of 'fads' and 'fashions' acts as a rebuke to Hilmer and Donaldson. It suggests that the contemporary dismissal of 'fads' as ideas and innovations that are ephemeral, insubstantial and so unworthy of sustained scrutiny indulges the understanding that fads require nothing of practitioners beyond mindless imitation. This is a point to which we will return. For the moment, however, we must continue with our review of redemptionist texts.

The witch doctors

The text prepared by Micklethwait and Wooldridge (1997) is perhaps less strident than that of Hilmer and Donaldson (1996), yet it is no more forthcoming on the nature of 'fads'. These commentators, it is worth noting, do not really speak of gurus. They talk instead of 'witch doctors' who, like the poets of an earlier age, are said to be 'the unacknowledged legislators of mankind . . . laying down the law, reshaping institutions, refashioning our language and, above all, reorganising people's lives' (5). The presence of these 'legislators of mankind' is not, however, a cause for celebration because the witch doctors, they tell us, offer forms of analysis that are 'constitutionally incapable of self-criticism' (15). Thus Micklethwait and Wooldridge suggest that the witch doctors develop and apply forms of expression that act to limit analytical reflection and development.

It is true of course that all specialist groupings tend to develop their own specialist forms of expression. Yet when a specialist in maxillo-facial surgery (for example) chooses to describe a trauma involving 'a non-displaced fracture of the left zygoma in a healthy adolescent', this will offer her col-leagues (if not the patient) a very clear account of the issues that they may expect to face in clinic. The jargon developed by the witch doctors, and which now circulates widely in organised contexts, is, however, marked by ambiguity (while appearing to possess clarity) and is generalised (while appearing to target specific issues). For example, the (apparent) consen-sus developed when someone voices the suggestion that *going forward, we must now ensure the proactive development of a user interface that will enable an empowered culture of quality which exceeds expectations* exists only because all involved are, in the absence of any additional qualifica-tion, free to define 'empowerment', 'culture', 'service users' and 'expecta-tions' to reflect their own narrow interests and concerns. Little wonder, then, that Micklethwait and Wooldridge complain that the 'witch doctors' are a menace to managers and to the organisations which they steward. And yet despite what appears to be a blanket dismissal of the witch doctors, Mick-lethwait and Wooldridge suggest that there are some among this grouping who offer sound advice. Thus Drucker is 'good' while Hammer is 'bad'. Similarly 'knowledge work' is presented as a thoroughly sound idea while 'globalisation' is mocked as a management concept.

This more conditional appreciation of the witch doctors suggests, how-ever, the presence of underlying analytical problems that Micklethwait and Wooldridge have failed to realise. For example, we might suggest that the authors' support for Drucker and their dismissal of Hammer demonstrates not discernment but a degree of 'flexing' which serves only to highlight the limits of personification! Similarly, we might suggest that the endorsement of 'knowledge work' (see Collins, 1997) and the simplistic dismissal of 'globalisation' (see Collins, 2000) might be said to signal a deeper igno-rance of history and (despite protestations to the contrary) a failure to engage in the form of sustained analytical reflection that might demonstrate why both of these rhetorical projections deserve to be taken seriously. Thus the redemptionist ambition of Micklethwait and Wooldridge appears to be half-hearted and is like that of Hilmer and Donaldson: *anti-management* because, aside from labelling managers as dopy and ill-educated, they have no robust explanation as to why managers might be drawn to that which they have dismissed as words full of sound and fury, signifying nothing!

The work of Brindle and Stearns (2001) is like that of Hilmer and Don-aldson, broadly redemptive in nature and in character. It is, however, richer than the redemptive texts considered thus far and has, as we shall see, a more developed sense of historical matters. These welcome and worthy characteristics ensure that the work of Brindle and Stearns eschews the sim-ple-minded managerialism that is the hallmark of the hagiologists *and* the deeper traps that await their fellow redemptionists. Thus where Hilmer and

Donaldson rail against the damage which 'fads' to do 'our corporations', Brindle and Stearns remain sceptical about the use of the first person plural in this context. Indeed, their analysis prompts reflection on a number of assumptions (and refrains) which bolster the hagiologies and which quietly underpin the claims made by their fellow redeemers. When it comes time to weigh the merits of guru theory, therefore, Brindle and Stearns employ a form of calculus, which (uniquely within this category) recognises the sectional nature of organisations and the local character of interests. For Brindle and Stearns, therefore, guru theory acquires an audience and a marketplace because it may:

1   Help to provide a sense of common identity. Thus Brindle and Stearns suggests that guru theory is potent because it retains the ability to foster the sense of cohesion which, hagiologies assume, naturally prevails.
2   Encourage organisational isomorphism and in so doing enhance organisational legitimacy. Elaborating upon this point, Brindle and Stearns suggest that organisations which embrace industry-wide innovations such as re-engineering and/or culture change may reduce investor and customer anxiety insofar as these developments ensure that organisations in similar markets look and act alike. Combining points one and two, Brindle and Stearns (2001) suggest that the 'fads' and 'fashions' prevalent within the business world 'permit conformity under the guise of novelty and independence, and all the while give voice and identity' (7) to managerial ambition.
3   Allow managers to engage in public demonstrations of activity, energy and, perhaps more importantly, vision.
4   Provide avenues for career development. Thus Brindle and Stearns remind us that these days you can become 'VP Quality', the 'Head of Customer Satisfaction' or a 'Czar' of some kind!
5   Help managers to communicate in culturally appropriate ways through the development and dissemination of a common language built upon shared referents such as 'culture', 'quality', 'empowerment' and 'stakeholders'.
6   Open new communications channels for the discussion of hot topics and salient issues.
7   Provide legitimation for certain courses of action that may otherwise prove problematic. Noting this, Collins (2000) argues that 'downsizing' and its cousin, 'rightsizing', provide managers with a means of talking about mass dismissal which makes this process unavoidable and faceless. Indeed, Collins suggests that the rhetoric of downsizing absolves managers from responsibility for initiating this action while distancing them from its human and civic consequences.

Recognising the complexity of organisations and the inherent plurality of organisational life, therefore, Brindle and Stearns offer a rational (if politically motivated) reading of guru theory. Their analysis suggests that guru theory cannot damage 'our' organisations because this collective fiction does not exist. Organisations, their analysis suggests, are more usefully understood as constellations of competing orientations and concerns (Collins, 1998). The redemptionist account of Brindle and Stearns therefore avoids the suggestion that managers are simply dopy and have been duped by the gurus into accepting fads that damage *the* organisation. Instead the authors recognise that in a competitive arena where investors, the board, colleagues and customers hold certain expectations as to organisational form, function and performance, guru theory provides a means of building a career while addressing the concerns and anxieties of significant stakeholders. Yet while Brindle and Stearns are prepared to offer an olive branch to the actors who have been traduced by Hilmer and Donaldson, they show no such succour to *Harvard Business Review*. Indeed, they suggest that this journal has done much to promote guru theory and should now be held to account for some of the wilder excesses which guru theory has visited upon the business world and upon civic life more generally.

Reflecting upon the manner in which HBR has acted to prepare the way for guru theory, Brindle and Stearns (2001) observe that this journal changed direction in the 1970s. At this time, they suggest, a new editorial policy was put in place which made a legitimate space for guru theory in commercial life. There were, they tell us, 'three main tacks' (60) in this shift of course:

1   A 'significant shift away from an historical, philosophical grounding toward a decidedly ahistorical bent' (60–61).
2   A retreat from those perspectives which attempted to place the consideration of management in a social and economic context.
3   The development of a self-help ethos which meant that 'speed [in action] and [analytical] simplification became virtues' (63).

Yet having offered this distinctive historical-political critique, Brindle and Stearns – in a bizarre and frustrating turn – fall back into line with the redemptionists noted earlier. Thus they insist that guru theory can be tamed by careful (professional) management. Quite who or what will provide this 'professional management' is of course never fully elaborated. Indeed, despite noting the rhetorical power and appeal of the gurus, Brindle and Stearns choose a rather simplistic counter-rhetoric which takes refuge in 'common-sense' (see Collins, 1996). Thus Brindle and Stearns suggest that we may apply guru theory usefully and safely *if* we take steps to address the more fanciful components of the rhetoric which the gurus employ:

Pour in a need for change to deal with problems old and new. Add a sense of perspective, distilled from an understanding of what faddism is all about and what the long-standing issues are. Stir in common sense. The result: It's possible to use fads without being faddist.

(206)

With a small half-step, therefore, we find ourselves once more in the company of Micklethwait and Wooldridge (1997) as we are dispatched to sniff out the 'good' fads in a cocktail swimming with 'bad' ideas. The problem being, of course, that in the absence of a recipe – in the absence of a useful analytical frame which reflects upon the nature of management and upon the structure of our organised worlds – the advice offered by Brindle and Stearns remains very limited.

The agnostics of the guru industry

As you might expect, it can be difficult to grasp quite what it is that the 'agnostics' of the guru industry believe. The writers of the hagiologies clearly 'believe in' the gurus. The 'redeemers', meanwhile, protest (albeit half-heartedly) that they believe in management and would save managers from the clutches of the self-serving gurus. But what do the 'agnostics' believe?

Agnostics, generally, believe that material matters are all that we can know. Thus agnostics would argue that the value of 'faith' and the wisdom of 'having faith', which is stressed in religious teaching, is highly questionable. Similarly, the 'agnostics' of the 'guru industry' reject guru theorising because it is, they warn us, based upon faith and belief rather than upon truth and proof.

Huczynski's *Management Gurus* (1993), discussed in some detail in chapter two, remains, perhaps, the key agnostic text. Huczynski's analysis of the teachings of the gurus is therefore different to that voiced by the redemptionists. Huczynski is, frankly, really not very interested in discussing whether guru ideas are good for corporations. Framing the key problematic in this manner would be to indulge the suggestion that organisations are in fact built upon a common understanding of means and ends. Instead, Huczynski is keen to understand the manner in which guru theory (whether 'good, 'bad' or otherwise) is constituted and secures its effects.

Having offered an extended analysis of Huczynski's work in chapter two, there is little to be gained from repeating ourselves. Instead we will offer an account of Kieser's (1997) work, which in chapter two was granted only a very brief mention. Kieser's contribution is, as we shall see, worthy of sustained analysis because it offers a critical review of Abrahamson's (1996) neo-institutional account of fads and fashions.

Kieser's 'agnostic' analysis

Reflecting upon Abrahamson's (1996) analysis, Kieser (1997) suggests that there are reasons to doubt its neo-institutional credentials. Neo-institutional theory insists that organisations exist within 'fields'. These fields are defined by the existence of expectations, regulations and sanctions which encourage organisational isomorphism. Thus neo-institutional thinking suggests that organisations tend to develop similar structures and policies because they expect that conformity to such demands will enhance legitimacy, and in so doing, ensure their continuing survival.

Building upon this understanding, Abrahamson suggests that managers are now expected to embrace new managerial ideas because they must demonstrate their personal commitment to 'norms of progress'. Kieser (1997) accepts that this is a plausible suggestion. Yet he observes that this mechanism is not easily accommodated within neo-institutional thinking. Expanding upon this point, Kieser notes that neo-institutional thinking is centrally concerned with those stable expectations which promote (and reward) isomorphism whereas Abrahamson's (1996) 'norms of progress' make for change, instability and so heterogeneity. Thus Kieser (1997: 53) argues that Abrahamson's analysis remains not 'institutional' but 'aesthetic':

> Linking the hypothesis that managers have to adhere to norms of progress with neo-institutional theory . . . smacks of an attempt to create the impression that the explanation of the dynamics of management fashion does not rest on just one single hypothesis but on a highly reputed theory.

Looking more closely at the dynamics of the fashion-setting industry developed by Abrahamson, Kieser complains that his contemporary tends to ignore core elements of the model he has developed. Reflecting upon the dynamics of this fashion industry, Abrahamson notes that it has a supply-side and a demand-side. The supply-side, he suggest, is served by gurus, business schools, editors and publishers (among others) who collectively enable the development and dissemination of management knowledge. The demand-side, he suggests, is populated by management practitioners (broadly constituted) who demand innovations in response to 'techno-economic' concerns and 'sociopsychological' factors. In this context a 'techno-economic' factor might, for example, relate to an innovative form of technology that would remove or reduce the number of individuals needed to staff the huge order-fulfilment warehouses that now exist on the edges of our cities and towns. The sociopsychological factors outlined by Abrahamson are, in contrast, synonymous with the 'norms of progress' outlined earlier.

Abrahamson argues that techno economic factors and sociopsychological issues compete to shape the demand for management fashion. Yet if this is correct, it is a very one-sided competition since Kieser notes that Abrahamson pays attention only to the sociopsychological dimensions of his model. This process and outcome, Kieser suggests, serve to reaffirm the suggestion that Abrahamson's is an aesthetic argument masquerading as a neo-institutional model.

Turning his attention from Abrahamson's demand-side concerns to consider supply-side dynamics, Kieser suggests that Abrahamson misunderstands, and so misrepresents, organisational rhetorics. Thus Kieser complains that Abrahamson argues that organisational fashion-setters are said, first, to sense incipient practitioner preferences and having sensed these are then said to articulate persuasive rhetorics. This phased approach, Kieser argues, diminishes rhetoric and relegates it to a subsidiary concern; a matter of embellishment. Objecting to this relegation, Kieser insists that rhetoric is central to all forms of communication and needs to be accorded its proper position in discourse whether this be (primarily) literary, political or scientific in its orientation and appeal.

Objecting to Abrahamson's (1996) neo-institutional assertions, therefore, Kieser outlines an alternative analysis which builds upon an appreciation of 'fashion' and 'rhetoric' to offer a more explicit and more fully elaborated analysis of the aesthetics of management fashion. In common with Huczynski, Kieser suggests that managerial innovations will tend to enjoy greater success when they conform more fully to the rhetorical ideas, which he suggests characterise guru theory. Thus Kieser advocates what amounts to a 10-point rhetorical ideal for guru theorising, which accommodates more fully the appreciation of fashion and aesthetics advanced by Abrahamson.

1   Kieser suggest that guru ideas are more persuasive, more rhetorically powerful, when they build their manifestos upon the existence of a single idea or absent component which will deliver as yet unrealised benefits. Guru rhetorics are more powerful, therefore, when/where they articulate a simple idea – such as 'quality', 'reengineering' or 'culture change' – which in execution promises to resolve the problematic issue of the moment.

2   Successful ideas, Kieser observes, tend to assert that they are indispensable (as in point one) and unavoidable. This unavoidability may arise due to changes in technology, changes in regulation, changes in the competitive landscape (for example) or indeed due to changes in all three. In short, Kieser argues that successful guru ideas are wedded to TINA.

3   There are certain ideas and orientations which in polite society decent people are expected (variously) to support or denounce. Writing about industrial relations, for example, McInnes (1989) observes the manner in which neo-liberal policies challenged the cross-party political consensus that had shaped British policy in the post-World War II period. Noting that managers and politicians had attacked Britain's trades unions for being inflexible, McInnes highlights the manner in which this rhetoric placed workers and their unions at a considerable disadvantage. He observes that in polite society it is, in effect, forbidden to be *against* 'flexibility'. To voice concerns about flexibility, McInnes observed is to side with 'rigidity' and 'autarky'. Discussing 'empowerment', Collins (1994) raises a similar concern. To be *against* empowerment, he observes, is to come out *for* Taylorism and against democracy. Recognising the rhetorical appeal of key concepts prized within developed Western societies, Kieser argues that guru theory has a distinct rhetorical advantage whenever it is harnessed to concepts such as 'democracy' or 'freedom', which are valued intrinsically.

4   Kieser argues that guru theory demands some level of change. But guru theory, he argues, does not appear before us as an instruction manual. Rather, it is exhortative. It highlights the possibility of outstanding solutions developed in the presence of and thanks to the conduct of individuals who, in behaving extraordinarily, are to be considered exemplars. Echoing this appreciation of the nature of guru theorising, Kociatkoewicz and Kostera (2016) suggest that it might be framed as a literary genre; a codification of discursive properties which in the absence of detailed instructions offers managers a sense of identity, which demands energy and action.

5   Guru theory suggests the availability of new ideas. Yet while new ideas have an intrinsic appeal to those who must work within politically-charged contexts, Kieser warns us that those ideas and concepts, represented as novel, need to be framed in a manner that disparages neither the 'old' ideas nor those who prosecuted these. Thus Kieser suggest that the architects of guru theory need to make it clear that the old ideas worked . . . in that time and in those places where they were pursued. In this respect, the core rhetorical challenges facing the gurus is to establish that changes in the competitive landscape (rehearsed at point two) now require new forms of thinking and action.

6   Guru ideas combine simplicity and ambiguity. This combination, in practice, ensures that it is easy to voice broad public support for a new initiative while applying this locally and in a distinctive manner.

7   Guru ideas are simply rendered but they are, it is said, rather more difficult to implement. Yet this warning is, Kieser suggests, a form of

marketing for it makes it clear to the would-be purchaser that it is the best and the brightest who will be the pioneers. To be an early-adopter is therefore to demonstrate possession of 'the right stuff' (Wolfe, 1979).

8   Guru theory is not to be confused with academic theorising. Unlike academic texts, guru theory does not *show its working*. It is untroubled by the niceties of methods, methodologies, and cares not a jot for the reproduction of research results. Instead, it secures its authority through the exhibition of 'persuasive examples' (Lischinsky, 2008).

9   Kieser is at pains to demonstrate that guru theory is rhetorical at its root and in its expression. The same, of course, could be said of all texts . . . including this one! What makes guru theory distinctive as a literary genre, however, is its construction in and through short sentences which, while they may be acronym-heavy, demonstrate a limited vocabulary that is free of those complex ideas which we are accustomed to seeing in academic texts.

10 The success of guru texts may be enhanced by good marketing. But no amount of marketing will sustain a text that is somehow ignorant of the demand-side characteristics which prevail within the market for management knowledge. Sometimes, as we saw in chapter two, the necessary congruence between supply-side and demand-side conditions may arise as the consequence of good, old-fashioned dumb luck. And we should not, I suggest, seek to diminish this factor. Wolfe's'(1979) account of the *Mercury* and *Apollo* space programmes makes it plain that those who demonstrated 'the right stuff' had the opportunity to do so because, at times in their lives when, for example, apparently doomed by a 'flat spin', they had 'lucked out'.

Furusten's (1999) analysis of popular management books shows a similar concern for rhetoric and, like Abrahamson (1996), demonstrates similar levels of misapprehension. Furusten's approach however does neatly encapsulate the issue that marks the boundary between the redemptionist and the agnostic contributions to the guru industry.

Both the redemptionists and the agnostics, we should acknowledge, recognise that gurus trade in representations of the world of business which claim to be both real and substantive. Yet where the redemptionists construct an essentialist account wherein the gurus are said to produce rhetorical falsehoods, Furusten insists that the representations constructed by the gurus *are* substantial, *do* have material consequences and as such *should* be taken seriously. Thus Furusten tells us that, like Huczynski (1993), his aim is to 'characterise not criticise popular management' (1999: 12). Yet Furusten insists that his work challenges and extends the work of his contemporary. Thus while Huczynski is, he tells us, content to offer an empirical analysis of the post-production influence of guru theory on managerial thought and action, Furusten's stated concern is to consider the manner in which popular management is produced, diffused and consumed. In this regard, Furusten is concerned to know *what* guru theory is and *how* it achieves its effects.

I rather like Furusten's analysis. Truthfully, it has done much to shape my own reflections on the consumption of popular management ideas (see Collins, 2004, 2012a). But I do believe that he exaggerates the differences between his contribution and that of Huczynski. Indeed, I believe that Furusten is putting his shoulder to an open door when he voices this criticism because Huczynski is, I suggest, very much aware that guru theorising is made, spread and applied within contexts which, in being notable for complexity, actively encourage translation and adaptation. That said, there are components of Furusten's analysis which are distinctive and which, in the context of this 'research overview', do merit further reflection and elaboration.

In common with Abrahamson (1996), Furusten places his analysis of 'fads' within an institutional context. He does not quite advocate the presence of 'norms of progress'. Nonetheless, he does suggest that organisational life is shaped by three broad sets of influence or pressure, these influences being coercive pressures, mimetic pressures and normative pressures. These three sets of influence, individually or collectively, make for organisational isomorphism. Applying this appreciation of the dynamics shaping our organised lives to the arena of management fashion, Furusten suggests that popular management/guru theory is significant because it acts to enable key innovations, which increasingly underscore key the reproduction of social order. Thus Furusten suggests that guru theory acts coercively, mimetically and normatively to engineer change.

Reflecting upon such coercive pressures, for example, Furusten's analysis would tend to indicate that consultants retained by the UK Treasury (for example) have acted to shape the structure and conduct of UK financial institutions (and the conduct of their auditors) thanks to the development and implementation of a risk-based, 'light-touch' regulatory environment for UK financial services.

Commenting upon mimetic pressures, Furusten's analysis encourages us to consider those consultant-led initiatives which have encouraged organisations to decentralise to become 'lean' and 'agile'. And finally on normative pressures, Furusten's analysis suggests that we might pay attention to the lobby concerns, which nowadays oblige employers to demonstrate that they are 'family-friendly', 'disability-aware' and 'socially-responsible', act to enable 'the reproduction of social order'.

Turning his attention from 'what' popular management has wrought to the issue of 'how' it has secured its outcomes, Furusten calls upon the work of Latour (1987). Latour is perhaps best known for his work on the development of technology and for his reflections on the work undertaken by scientific collectives. It would be wrong, however, to limit Latour's purview to the consideration of laboratory life. Indeed, it would be more apposite to suggest that Latour is concerned to understand the manner in which experts (of all varieties) come together to build worlds in our name.

Examining the manner in which experts toil to construct knowledge in a form that facilitates its diffusion, Latour observes that ideas acquire the quality of 'portability' when they are a) 'textualised' (that is rendered in a fashion that allows them to be written down and spoken of beyond the immediate locus of their production) and b) arrayed in a manner which moves the reader/audience quickly 'downstream' *from* an initially questionable or controversial declaration *to* an end-point where all concepts and components necessary to the argument are arranged in a fashion which obliges the reader/audience simply to accept the author's preferred world view. In this respect the ambition of the guru is, Furusten suggests, to develop a 'black box'; a shared appreciation of the world and its problems that is so convincing that it is accepted tacitly and in silence.

Furusten suggests that this 'black boxing' of the world is facilitated within popular management by a mode of representation which builds and depends upon a form of metaphorical expression that is developed in and through fragmentary declarations. This is an interesting observation. Indeed, anyone with a nodding acquaintance with popular management will, I am sure, readily concede that it trades in *bon mots*, pithy asides, acronyms and anecdotes. Yet we must be careful. Metaphor is, as we suggested earlier, often misunderstood and/or misrepresented within organisations. It is therefore worth pausing to look more deeply at the concerns which arise when metaphor in guru theorising is subject to academic scrutiny.

Furusten's (1999) observation that guru texts trade in metaphorical fragments is, of course, quite correct. Yet in voicing this opinion Furusten is, despite his stated desire to characterise rather than to criticise popular management, actually voicing a complaint. His complaint, simply put, is that gurus use literary embellishment to obscure the extent to which their knowledge claims or, if you prefer, the structure of their world-building endeavours lack an empirical foundation.

Grant and Oswick (1996), who have done much to enhance our understanding of metaphor in organised contexts, confirm and yet qualify Furusten's analysis. Thus the analysis developed by Grant and Oswick suggests that popular management is powerful *not* despite its dependence on metaphor (fragmentary or otherwise) but because it is built squarely upon this form expression. Yet to grasp fully the significance of this point, we may need to reconfigure our understanding of the manner in which metaphor acts to generate understanding.

Generative metaphor

Grant and Oswick (1996) remind us that dictionaries and primers on the craft of writing generally assert that metaphors are literary embellishments which invite a direct comparison between otherwise distinct elements of the world. In my home town for example, mothers would regularly complain that their children were 'house devils and street saints'. In the academic world, Morgan (1986) has offered an extended analysis of prevailing organisational metaphors. He suggests that social organisations may be described *as* organisms, machines or psychic prisons, to name but three available metaphors of organisation.

Furusten's (1999) misgiving as to the application of metaphor in popular management grasps, at one level, the power and prevalence of such figures of speech. And yet he seems to share the concern voiced by Pinder and Bourgeois (1982: 643) that metaphors should be considered to be problematic in domains that would make claims to objective knowledge. Thus Pinder and Bourgeois complain that metaphors have no rightful place in the domain of (social) science because they are 'stated in terms that do not have enough clear content to be falsifiable'. This objection, however, tends to indulge the suggestion that there are certain genres which might be liberated from metaphor and in freeing themselves from this burden would become clearer; more scientific; properly objective. The problem being that metaphor is so central to all modes of communications that we cannot, in truth, get by without it. In this regard metaphor, far from being a wordsmith's frippery, is more usefully considered to be a way of thinking. Indeed, Grant and Oswick argue that metaphor has a generative capacity; the ability to provoke news ways of seeing, new forms of understanding. This understanding suggests that if the fragmentary metaphors of popular management are problematic, they are so because they act to limit our capacity to reimagine organisational processes and organised outcomes. This is a point usefully elaborated by Dunford and Palmer (1996).

Reflecting upon the deployment of metaphor in the study of organisation and change, Dunford and Palmer highlight the manner in which deep or underlying metaphors phrased in terms of the body, for example, have enabled a distinctive discourse of restructuring. Indeed, they observe that organic metaphors of the organisation – as body – have allowed authors to suggest (and demand) an end to 'corporate obesity', a need for slimming remedies and, at the extremity of this mode of expression, a need for surgical intervention which would excise those elements of the organisation deemed to be flabby

Acknowledging that other metaphors are available to those who would shape our organisational futures, Dunford and Palmer note that executives *might* have been constituted as corporate bakers (rather than corporate surgeons), artfully combining ingredients and nurturing effervescent reactions! Crucially, therefore, Dunford and Palmer remind us that metaphors are powerful because they direct *and* divert. Thus metaphors illuminate yet they can blind us in their light obscuring (generative) alternatives. We would do well, therefore, to note that to speak of stakeholders is not to speak of 'carpet-baggers'. To speak of 'clans' (see Deal and Kennedy, 1982) is surely to identify 'outsiders' who, because they fail to think, look or act like us, do not merit the privileges associated with full membership of the collective. Similarly, we might acknowledge that to invoke the root metaphor of 'journey' is to enable a discussion of 'steering', 'direction' and of 'cow-paths' that need to be paved and other blockages that need to be overcome (see Hammer, 1990). And finally, we should concede that to laud leadership is to avoid speaking of other organised realities suggested for example by Morgan's (1986) 'snake pit'!

Jackson (1996, 2001) also draws our attention the rhetorical construction of guru theory. Like Furusten, Jackson invites us to develop an awareness of the manner in which such accounts of the contemporary problems of management secure their meaning and exercise their effects. Jackson's work is, therefore, usefully described as 'agnostic'. Yet where Furusten (1999) and Huczynski (1993) deal with the broad canvas of popular management, Jackson focuses upon three core representations: business process re-engineering (advanced by Hammer (1990)); the effectiveness movement (led by Stephen Covey (1989)); and the learning organisation (as constituted by Peter Senge (1990)).

Drawing upon Burrell's (1997) suggestion that we think *with* rather than *about* our beliefs, Jackson argues that we follow the gurus because they mobilise our deeper fears *and* the motivations that stem from our identities. Yet Jackson's (agnostic) contribution is distinctive because he suggests that the gurus mobilise rhetorical visions or, if you will, 'fantasy themes'. These fantasy themes, Jackson argues, breathe life into the worlds and endeavours that the gurus would construct in our names. Echoing an idea previously rehearsed in our treatment of the redemptionists, Jackson suggests that the gurus act not as organisational scientists dispassionately rendering the world, but as playwrights and storytellers who work to challenge; to deconstruct and then manufacture anew what it means to be a skilful leader, a useful manager, a good employee.

Focusing attention on business process reengineering (BPR), however, Jackson (1996) voices misgivings about the violent imagery that has been used to convey core elements of popular management. BPR, he warns us, will visit upon employees the forced marches that characterised the Nazi treatment of those herded to concentration camps and the Soviet treatment of prisoners of war. Indeed, and lest anyone doubt the violence of this period of history (or the zeal of Hammer), Jackson pauses to remind us that the advocates of BPR promise to shoot those who fall behind or who step out of line!

This violent metaphor is, of course, vile and dehumanising. Perhaps one of the very few positive thoughts that can be voiced when faced with this representation of the world is that it makes the root metaphor of corporate dieting and calorie control seem benign. Yet Jackson's analysis does serve to remind us that BPR has attracted an audience (despite the offence to my sensibilities) because it:

- Triggers a basic instinct for self-preservation insofar as it threatens the continuing existence of all forms of business organisation.
- Offers those who have been found wanting the prospect of redemption in and through BPR.
- Reconstructs the convert to BPR as someone truly worthy of salvation.

My lamentations on the violent imagery of BPR offer, I suggest, a useful means to separate 'agnostic' and 'atheistic' submissions to the guru industry. This division, I believe, turns upon what those who have witnessed and/or revealed the rhetoric of popular management then do with this revelation. In this regard, the division between the 'agnostics' and the 'atheists' of the guru industry turns upon the response(s) offered to a set of key questions:

- Is it enough merely to know (of) the world? Or having come to understand the world in all its imperfection is there an obligation to act?
- Having constructed an argument which says, for example, that BPR succeeds rhetorically because it constructs a way of thinking about the world that is violently dehumanising is there a duty to intervene to act against this?
- Having revealed the extent to which salvation is earned through the sacrifice of those left behind or summarily dispatched *en route*, is there an obligation to do more than report its structure?

I do not intend to answer these questions for you. Only you can answer these questions, of course. Nonetheless, the existence of such questions mark, I suggest, the point at which agnostic commentaries fall silent and the point at which the atheists of the guru industry make their presence felt. Let us proceed to look in more depth at the questions raised by the 'atheists' of the 'guru industry'.

The atheists of the guru industry

The first iteration of the 'guru industry' which I developed (see Collins, 2000) suggested that the atheistic segment of this collective might be considered to be occupied by a form of anti-management scholarship. This assertion, while not incorrect, was potentially misleading because it failed either to acknowledge or indeed to explore the many different ways in which those who harbour serious reservations about guru theorising and its effects might articulate their concerns. In a more recent treatment of the 'guru industry' (Collins, 2019), I suggested the need for a broader and more inclusive account of the atheistic segment of the 'guru industry'. Thus I highlighted the strained co-existence of labour process scholars and postmodernists of all persuasions within this node. This was a useful qualification. Yet even this modification, I now realise, remains too restrictive because it is too focused upon managerial matters, whereas a more developed response to guru theorising would usefully build upon a broader concern with matters political, ecological and educational.

In this section I will suggest that while 'anti-management' scholars are indeed present and, legitimately, active within the atheistic segment of the 'guru industry', this portion of the continuum is broader than previously suggested. Unlike the hagiologists who celebrate the wisdom of *the* gurus and the redemptionists and agnostics who (albeit in slightly different ways) would work to enhance organisational processes and outcomes by challenging the gurus, the atheists, I now realise, have an agenda that lifts our eyes beyond the local and the narrowly managerial to invite and to provide a radical reconsideration of (for example) politics, ethics, education and environmental matters. Unlike earlier iterations of the 'guru industry', therefore, the atheistic portion of the continuum revealed and rendered here offers what amounts to a radical political-economy of guru theorising.

In an attempt to give a flavour of such atheistic renderings of the 'guru industry', I will offer brief reflections on Burrell's (1997) *Pandemonium*, Kostera's (2015) *Occupy Management* and Parker's (2018) *Shut Down the Business School*.

Pandemonium

Burrell's (1997) account of *Pandemonium*, which featured in the very earliest rendering of the 'guru industry' (Collins, 2000), invites a retro-organisational analysis. This mode of analysis, he tells us, has been designed to reveal and to rediscover ideas and orientations lost or obscured by the problematics which shape guru theorising. Selecting Charles Handy[4] as his *bête noir* (mainly, I suspect, because of the linguistic possibilities which this allows him as a keen student of language and humour), Burrell makes numerous references to limitations inherent in 'Handy Pocket Theory' (Burrell, 1997: 2) and to the attempts made by 'Handy Wipes' (85) to clean up, or to obscure, the true nature of organisation and our anxieties regarding organisational life. Yet where agnosticism leads to a focus upon the social-scientific, material world, Burrell presents us with a view of the material world which is profoundly anti-scientific (or at least anti-scientistic). In this sense Burrell's work, while clearly an attack upon the gurus of management, is atheistic because it demands to be read as a critique of the instrumentalism which the gurus encourage. To this end, his text is designed to shock our modern sensibilities which accept and indulge the idea that management as an elite cadre, and as a body of knowledge, is simply and plainly a 'good thing'. Thus Burrell observes that life is notable for its shit!

Discussing our cities, Burrell draws our attention to the amount of shit, both human and animal, which, in previous eras, would have been a feature of the city streets of London. Indeed, Burrell notes that during the hot summer months, the stench would be so foul that the wealthy city-dwellers would retreat to the country to escape the smell. It is worth observing, therefore, that while shit is a notable feature of life, life isn't shit – not for all anyway.

Readers may balk at my usage of the term shit (there, I have used it again). Some may find the term shocking and unnecessary. Yet this is exactly Burrell's point. He warns us that we neglect the 'profane' at our peril. He has therefore elected to focus upon that which is 'profane' in order to show the intellectual costs of our ignorance of 'shit'.

Building upon this analysis, Burrell argues that the gurus are appealing, and so popular, because they are only too willing to obscure the dark side; the shitty, profane aspects of the organisations which they would create. Yet he warns us that the 'Handy Wipes' of guru theory will not clean up the problems of organising and managing others which we now face. 'Handy Wipes' may, of course soothe the anxieties of organisational elites, but they will not, and cannot, alter the nature of the social organisation of production.

In an attempt to counter the chauvinistic tendencies of guru theorising, Burrell argues for a 'retro-organisation' theory which, he tells us, might be employed to reveal the (Kingdom of) 'Pandemonium' hidden within/ beneath the representations of managing and organising preferred by the gurus. Thus Burrell warns us that while the gurus focus upon globalisation (and on the salaried employees within these globalising corporations), peasants are now more numerous on the planet than they were in the year 1500! Indeed, he argues that peasant organisation might offer useful insights on contemporary issues. This is a point elaborated by Gray (1999).

Commenting upon the rhetoric and utility of the 'free market', Gray observes that since the 1980s governments in Britain and America have constructed their economic policies around *the need* to free markets from restriction, from regulation, from 'red tape'. Those of us who live in modern democratic societies are, as Kieser (1997) reminds us, rather taken by notions of freedom, choice and liberty. We are therefore inclined to accept 'free markets' – tacitly and silently (Latour, 1987) – as 'good things'. Gray warns us against this presumption. He suggests that free markets are far from the spontaneous formations represented in orthodox economic theorising. Indeed, he argues that so-called free markets must be engineered and maintained. Apparently 'free' markets therefore require significant amounts of governmental regulation and, associated with this, sizeable quantities of social and political engineering designed, for example, to ensure that the tax and benefit systems reward the wealthy while pushing the unemployed into paid (if precarious) employment.

Contrasting (so-called) free market situations with those developed by our ancestors, both Gray and Burrell suggest that our peasant forebears developed regulatory systems governing, for example, access to common land which were flexible, dynamic and sustainable. These regulations, they argue, endured through centuries because they were pragmatic and because they were founded upon social reciprocities. Unfortunately, free market economics has, through legislation, reduced economic exchange to a price mechanism and has, consequently, developed a short-term solution that places more and more of us (the hewers of wood) in 'the shit'. Burrell's knowledge of peasant organisation therefore leads him to advocate the overthrow of the gurus of management, not to improve 'our organisations', but to allow us to understand, more fully, that life when it is structured and organised around 'popular management' is pretty shitty.

Occupy Management

Kostera's (2015) *Occupy Management* has, perhaps, a less abrasive tone. But it is, like Burrell's *Pandemonium*, a very personal book which usefully communicates an atheistic perspective on the gurus. Kostera's text commences with a picture of the writer's grandfather and concludes fittingly enough with a picture of the author. Here, on the final page, Kostera peers into the sunlight and smiles at her readers. This smile has no teeth. This is not the 'eight-to-eight' smile of the red carpet.[5] Yet it remains a real smile; one delivered by the eyes.

Why have I begun to write in this manner? The answer is simple. I am following Kostera's instructions and in so doing I am honouring her approach which, as I interpret it, is a) to share ideas of self-organisation and, in so doing, b) to return the processes, practices and problematics of managing to those who have been subject to its imperial ambitions. In this there are clear echoes of Burrell's (1997) *Pandemonium*. Yet where Burrell's text crafts a passage to a forgotten history of guilds, common grazing and folk-knowledge, Kostera's text seeks a connection to the lived biographies and life experiences of her students and readers.

Occupy Management, perhaps unsurprisingly, channels concerns similar to those articulated by the Occupy Wall Street movement which, in September 2011, provided a focus for groups concerned to challenge economic inequality, political corruption and its more-or-less lawful counterpart, corporate lobbying. Kostera's text, of course, is not constituted as a direct attack on the gurus of management (although as we shall see it does have much to say about these actors and about the other components of the 'guru industry'), nor does it advocate public picketing, public demonstrations or the cyber-activism which became hallmarks of the Occupy Wall Street movement. Nonetheless, Kostera is keen to challenge the representations of working and managing which have come to us from the academy and, more recently, the gurus.

At root, Kostera's text offers a challenge to contemporary representations of management. She is therefore keen to overcome the excesses that in the guise of 'leadership' allow vanity to stand for vision and self-interest to trump community and ecology. Yet unlike the 'agnostics' of the 'guru industry', Kostera's core intention is to secure a radically different form of conduct and action which is rooted in and based upon (self) reflection. To advance this, Kostera offers poems, photographs and personal reflections designed to reveal a) the limits of those representations which now pass as 'good management' and b) to advance an alternative that in respecting plurality, reciprocity, community and ecology actively honours ideas of human decency.

Is this a romantic ideal? Yes, probably. But we should note that in this context the suggestion that realism trumps romance is the rhetorical weapon of an elite with vested interests. That Kostera's pedagogy uses poems and photography to encourage the development of new tales of self-management and self-organisation should not therefore be allowed to obscure the fact that this is a serious and intensely scholarly work. Indeed, in suggesting a reflexive response to the issues thrown up by such things as 'customer care' and 'best practice', *Occupy Management* advances the need for a form of social organisation which honours its inherent plurality. Thus Kostera's contribution to the field of management is welcome because it provides a useful counterpoint to the redemptionists and a challenge to the comfortable and socially detached agnostic (see also Kociatkiewicz and Kostera, 2016).

Shut Down the Business School

Parker's (2018) *Shut Down the Business School* offers, I suggest, a similarly atheistic contribution. Yet where Kostera's self-management philosophy articulates a discontent with the representations and codifications of management preferred by an academy, which remains distant and abstract,

Parker turns both barrels on the academy's most visible manifestation: the business school.

For Parker, the business school is at the heart of the modern malaise that the Occupy Movement was convened to address. This is not to suggest, of course, that the business school *actively* invites forms of conduct or somehow instructs ways of thinking that are obviously criminal. Yet Parker does suggest that ecological damage, criminality, inequality and poverty are societal outcomes for which the business school shares culpability. Putting flesh upon this suggestion, Parker suggests that through the development of a curriculum that is largely insensitive to plurality, and wilfully ignorant of ethical and ecological concerns, the business school enables a) ways of acting that are selfish and short-termist and b) modes of thinking that are chauvinistic.

The gurus of management, Parker suggests, are both product and process, organ and tool of the business school. Through their pronouncements and projections, he warns us, the gurus shape the organisation of these social formations and the curricula which they advance. This, of course, should not be taken as suggesting that all of those who work within the halls of the business school would advance or even endorse these agendas. It does, however, suggest that the prospects for reform from within are pitiful. Given this, Parker suggests that in order to oppose the gurus and the broader problems that their philosophies visit upon us, we should close the business school. This closure, he tells us, is necessary to secure an alternative realisation of the practices that shape universities, careers, community and the polity more generally.

Articulating the character of his preferred alternative to the business school, Parker unveils the School for Organising. This alternative, he tells us, will retain its location within the university but, unlike that which it will succeed, will be founded upon an assumption of organisational variety informed by an 'encyclopaedia of alternatives' (178). Furthermore, the evaluation of these alternatives will be shaped, he insists, not by some (supposedly) detached science of organisation, but by 'normative discussions' (178) designed to reveal and to test competing priorities organisational, political and ecological.

Does this make Parker's manifesto rhetorical? Of course it does! To claim otherwise would be to act in a politically self-serving manner. Indeed, to protest otherwise would be to advance a spuriously neutral morality of shareholder value that not even Tom Peters now takes seriously![6]

Parker's manifesto, like Kostera's, therefore, is not so much anti-management as pro-organisation. It rejects the shallow, unitary managerialism of the gurus and their hagiologists. In addition, it rejects the politically naïve but slightly more robust conceptualisation of the redemptionists. And since Parker's root concern is to characterise, to criticise *and* to secure change, it seems appropriate to suggest that his particular brand of materialism offers a useful contribution to that segment of the 'guru industry' that we have labelled 'atheistic'.

Concluding comments

This chapter has offered a revised and updated analysis of the 'guru industry' first outlined by Collins (2000). The present analysis differs from the initial rendering of the 'guru industry' in two key ways. Firstly the analysis of the 'guru industry', developed here, suggests four nodes: 'hagiologies'; 'redemptionist' texts; 'agnostic' accounts; and 'atheistic' analyses. Secondly, where previous iterations of the 'guru industry' tended to suggest that the atheistic node offered anti-management analyses of *the* gurus, the present iteration suggests that atheistic analyses of management's gurus are more usefully considered to be pro-organisation. Thus the atheists offer challenges to the representations preferred by the gurus and consider, variously, matters political, ecological and educational neglected by 'popular management'.

Taking account of these issues this chapter has offered an account of the hagiologies, the redemptionists, the agnostics and the atheistic nodes of the 'guru industry'. The dimensions of each node have been examined and the factors which discriminate one from another have been considered.

This chapter, of course, does not pretend to offer an exhaustive bibliography of responses to management's gurus. It does, however, produce a framework designed to allow readers to locate, to understand and to critique current and future responses to the gurus and their representations of the problems of management.

In the chapter that follows we move on from our analysis of 'guru theory' (considered in chapter two) and the 'guru industry' (rendered here) to offer critical reflections on guru performance or, as I have labelled this project, 'guru speak'(Greatbatch and Clark, 2005).

Notes

1 To offer but one example of this overlap: Carol Kennedy, whose work we discuss at various points throughout this text, also acts as a 'consulting editor'.
2 The initial iteration of the 'guru industry' (Collins, 2000) suggested that there were three groupings, but listed no fewer than five types of response. These contributions overlapped to some degree, of course, but I now accept that this headline discussion is perhaps a little confusing. In this revision, just four groupings are listed: hagiologies, redemptive texts, agnostic texts and atheistic texts.
3 This acronym is used to refer to Dead White European Males.

4 Charles Handy is often presented as one of only a few British gurus of management. Handy does, of course, reside in England, but he is Irish.

5 Dentists typically count teeth from the notional centre line of the mouth. Using
this calculus, there are eight teeth to the left of the centre line on the upper mandi-
ble and a further eight on the right side of the centre line. An 'eight-to-eight' smile
is that broad, toothy grin that reveals each and every one of the 32 teeth possessed
by the healthy adult.

6 In his Twitter feed, Peters now regularly rails against this and other systems of
measurement and reward.

5   Guru speak

Introduction

This chapter will essay a critical engagement with the analysis of guru performance developed by Clark and Greatbatch (2002, 2003; Greatbatch and Clark, 2003, 2005). While conceding a debt to the authors, this chapter will argue that the texts produced by Clark and Greatbatch continue to limit our understanding of what we might term 'the full circuit' of guru theorising (Collins, 2019). Indeed, we will argue that the texts prepared by Clark and Greatbatch offer a poor foundation for inquiry in this arena because they are beset by conceptual, methodological and empirical problems, which, while they are seriously limiting, remain largely unreported.

The chapter is structured as follows: We begin, necessarily, with a review of the account of 'guru speak' developed by Clark and Greatbatch. The second section will, therefore, introduce the work developed by the authors and will examine the manner in which their attempts to reconsider the work undertaken by management's gurus have altered our appreciation of *what gurus do*. In the third section of this chapter we will, however, reconsider the conceptualisation of the guru-performer developed by Clark and Greatbatch. We will argue that this conceptualisation is unstable, inconsistent and offers, consequently, a poor foundation for academic inquiry. In the fourth section, we will turn our attention to the methodology which the authors have developed to account for the stories told by the gurus during their stage performances. As we shall see, Clark and Greatbatch argue that these stories perform a pivotal role in guru performance. Stories, they tell us, act to secure and to maintain the affiliation of the audience. While accepting that this is a plausible account of the function that stories perform in this context, we will argue that Clark and Greatbatch have developed a definition of the nature of stories *and* an account of the practice of storytelling that is simply not fit for purpose. Our fifth section will build upon this analysis of methodology as we offer a critical review of the 'findings' generated by the authors. Here we will suggest that the authors, too, often fail to acknowledge the limitations of their data-set, and so make claims to knowledge that are, at best, in need of significant qualification and, at worst, simply unsupported. Finally we will conclude with a summary of our analysis, designed to preface the alternative analytical framework which we develop in chapter six as a response to the issues highlighted here.

What do gurus do?

What do management's gurus do?

This question, I imagine, will sound like a joke to many readers:

Gurus borrow your watch and then tell you the time.
Gurus prophesy futures that are already here.
Gurus boast about modesty.
Gurus speak Esperanto like natives.
Gurus . . . [insert your own witty and mildly disparaging comment here].

Yet the serious question remains: What, in fact, do gurus do?

Responding to this query, Clark and Greatbatch (2002) argue that academic commentaries on the gurus of management have developed only a very limited appreciation of what gurus do. Reviewing the academic response to management's gurus, the authors observe that academia has developed three lines of critique in its attempts to come to terms with the gurus of management.

The first of these strands, they observe, has focused narrowly upon the theoretical and/or conceptual building blocks which the gurus employ in their attempts to represent the contemporary problems of business and management. This line of critique, we should note, is simultaneously accurate and yet irrelevant because it is based upon a misunderstanding of what it is, in fact, that gurus do!

Taking up this point, Boltanski and Chiapello (2007) insist that the conceptual-methodological critiques of the gurus, which have been developed by academia, are based upon a fundamental misunderstanding of the function of guru theory. Gurus, they protest, do not seek to chronicle an empirical reality as academic critiques tend to assume. Rather, they exist to change our realities, and so marshal evidence in the form of persuasive examples (Lischinsky, 2008) to secure 'the engagement of a large number of actors whose zeal and conviction are decisive in the smooth running of firms' (Boltanski and Chiapello, 2007: 58).

The second strand of academic critique, Clark and Greatbatch (2002) observe, is based upon textual analyses and 'close readings' of the writings prepared by the gurus. These 'textual analyses', we should concede, are creative and have done much to refine our appreciation of the rhetorical strategies which the gurus employ to convince us of the saliency of their cause (see Furusten, 1999; Jackson, 2001). Nonetheless, Clark and Greatbatch argue that such treatments of guru theorising tend to reduce it to the written word and in so doing overlook or diminish the work that gurus must undertake in their seminars.

The third strand of academic critique in this arena, Clark and Greatbatch observe, is dedicated to the evaluation of guru theory in practice settings. These evaluations, we should concede, tend to be negative because guru theory seldom delivers on even a fraction of its promise. Yet Clark and Greatbatch (2002, 2003) suggest that such evaluations are largely inconsequential. Management's gurus, they argue, seldom act as conventional consultants. They do not generally work with managers to address and resolve organisational problems. Rather, the role of the gurus is more generalised; more abstract. They exist to reveal, justify and inspire the need for change. They do not deal in 'deliverables'. They do not in any real or meaningful sense take responsibility for 'change outcomes'. And they certainly do not engage in evaluation!

In a related, contemporary treatment of the subject of 'guru speak', Clark and Greatbatch (2003) offer a slightly different articulation of their professional discontents, which adds new lines of critique. Thus Clark and Greatbatch (2003) complain that academic appreciation of gurus and guru theorising assumes that the audience for guru theorising behaves passively and is largely docile in the hands of the gurus. In addition, they observe that academia has tended to assume that guru theorising is developed by special individuals who work in isolation to bring their special insights to the world. This point is also present (if less prominent) in the earlier iteration of 'guru speak' developed by Clark and Greatbatch (2002). Thus the authors observe that academics (and journalists) tend to depict gurus as 'lone creative geniuses [who] gain unique insights into modern organizational life by dabbling in their "organizational laboratories". They then emerge and use their expertise in rhetoric and persuasive communication to popularize their ideas through best-selling books and/or live presentations' (152–153). This 'great man' conceptualisation of the gurus, of course (see chapters two and three), overlooks the extent to which these actors build and depend upon a broader network of editors, ghost-writers, publicists and party-planners which has grown up to develop and to disseminate their wares.

Pulling these threads together, Clark and Greatbatch (2002, 2003) complain that academia's over-arching focus upon texts and the written word, its preoccupation with concepts and methods, and the associated neglect of empirical matters combined with its willingness to assume that the gurus are lone agents serving audiences which lack agency, has caused commentators to lose sight of what should be, surely, the central actor in this drama, namely, the management guru. In an attempt to place the guru centre-stage and in so doing to place the analysis of *what gurus do* on an empirical base, Clark and Greatbatch offer analyses of guru performance.

Commenting upon the significance of these performance events, Greatbatch and Clark (2005) argue that seminars 'are critical to [the gurus'] popularity and success' (16). Indeed, they observe that the appearance fees generated by these events 'can dwarf their book royalties' (16). Furthermore, they argue that stories and storytelling constitute the corner-stone of the guru seminar. Storytelling is, they tell us, the means by which the gurus secure and maintain the affiliation of the audience present.

While Clark and Greatbatch (2002) are plainly pioneers in this arena, they do concede that others have also acknowledged the important function which stories perform in guru theory. Thus Clark and Greatbatch note that others have sought to collect and collate the stories which the gurus reproduce in their texts. They are, however, dismissive of their contemporaries. Stories harvested from published sources are, they insist, blind to the complex social-political dynamics of storytelling, and so fail to recognise that speakers/storytellers are obliged a) to take steps to enrol the audience present and b) to secure their affiliation throughout the encounter. To remedy this neglect of the active audience, the authors analyse guru performance events with a view to exploring the rhetorical devices employed, the stories rendered and the role of humour.

The studies developed over time by the authors (Clark and Greatbatch, 2002, 2003; Greatbatch and Clark, 2003, 2005) build upon different datasets and pursue different (if closely related) themes. The presentation of the data, we should note, also changes and develops over time as the authors advance their research and agenda. For example, the text prepared by Clark and Greatbatch (2002) considers just two gurus (Tom Peters and Rosabeth Moss Kanter) and a total of five performance events, whereas the monograph produced by Greatbatch and Clark (2005) offers an analysis of performance events developed by four gurus (Tom Peters, Rosabeth Moss Kanter, Peter Senge and Gary Hamel). As the authors extend the scope of their studies, they also develop and refine the manner in which they reproduce their empirical materials. Thus in 2002 Clark and Greatbatch seem content merely to reproduce the words spoken by the gurus. Yet by 2005 the authors find it necessary to produce fuller transcripts of these performance events which detail pauses and hesitation as well as changes in intonation, volume and emphasis. Gestures and physical movements, we should note, are also recorded in this later text (Greatbatch and Clark, 2005) as the authors seek to account for aspects of performance that would be, otherwise, 'seen but unnoticed' (Clark and Greatbatch, 2002: 157). What remains constant across the analyses developed by the authors, however, is the desire to explore, empirically, the extent to which a) the oratory of the gurus and b) their success as shapers of opinion is related to c) the manner in which they package and deliver their ideas. Central to this empirical analysis is a consideration of the storytelling practices which the gurus invoke as they attempt to persuade us of their concerns.

Commenting upon the performance practices witnessed, Clark and Greatbatch (2002; Greatbatch and Clark, 2005) observe that gurus face three challenges as they take the stage.[1] Firstly they must act to enrol the audience present in the project that will unfold across the seminar event. Secondly the guru must take steps to sustain audience attention, within a context where there are few incentives so to do. Thirdly the authors suggest that if the guru is to develop an experience that is satisfactory for both presenter and audience, care must be taken to elicit affiliative responses from the audience.

Clark and Greatbatch observe that the primary affiliative response offered by the audience in this context is laughter. In addition, they observe that it is through storytelling that the guru most reliably secures this response. Accounting for this assertion, the authors concede that stories constitute but a minority of the speech created by the gurus. Yet they argue that such segments of talk are special because they account for the majority of the laughter events precipitated. Building upon this analysis, Clark and Greatbatch assert that the success of the performance events offered by the gurus of management largely hinges upon the practice of storytelling.

There is much to recommend the manifesto developed by Clark and Greatbatch. It is true that much of the academic inquiry developed on management's gurus has been based upon conceptual-methodological analyses. It is also accurate to suggest that this conceptual-methodological critique often tends to misunderstand the nature of guru theorising and its appeal. Furthermore, it is fair to suggest that our understanding of *what gurus do* has been shaped by ideas, arguments and understandings which have not been (in)formed empirically.

And yet there are problems with the research agenda developed and prosecuted by Clark and Greatbatch. Indeed – their core insights notwithstanding – there remain conceptual, methodological and empirical problems which, as we will learn, continue to limit our understanding of *what gurus do*. The remainder of this chapter will explore these issues and in so doing will lay the groundwork for the alternative formulation of the guru-as-performer that we will develop in chapter six.

Conceptualising the guru

Clark and Greatbatch, as we have seen, suggest that there is a need to recognise the contribution which seminar performances make to the market profiles of management's gurus. These seminar events, they tell us, are quite unlike guru texts. They are interactive and dynamic events, which require the guru to manage the sentiments of the audience and, crucially, their own public representations of self.

The authors understand that they are not the first to acknowledge the significance of the seminar events offered by the gurus of management. Indeed, Greatbatch and Clark (2005) acknowledge the existence of two analyses which they tell us pre-date their own efforts.[2] They complain, however, that academia has tended to assume that gurus act like religious evangelists when they take the stage. Huczynski's (1993) pioneering analysis of management's gurus is, they suggest, the foundation of this deep-seated misapprehension. Thus they argue that Huczynski's suggestion as to the *modus operandi* of the gurus is misleading because it builds upon Lewin's (1947) force-field analysis and in so doing suggests that the gurus operate in three movements, creating firstly a sense of anxiety within the audience before moving to induce a conversion to new forms of thought and action which, in the third phase of the encounter, is cemented 'permanently' in order to 'fix and fortify their converts' (Clark and Greatbatch, 2002: 154).[3]

The position adopted by the authors on the identity of the gurus and upon their ability to win 'converts', however, seems to change over time. Clark and Greatbatch (2002), for example, seem to adopt an approach to this issue that is data-led. In their 2002 text, therefore, the authors seem to build directly upon their empirical observations. They suggest that Rosabeth Moss Kanter brings a calm deportment to her seminars and contrast this with the evangelising approach adopted by Tom Peters. Offering a vivid illustration of Peters' conduct, *The Economist* (September 24, 1994: 73) some 25 years ago observed that Tom Peters causes 'middle managers to gape in awe' as he strides around the stage 'arms flailing, brow sweating, voice hoarse'.

By 2005, however, the position of the authors seems to have hardened on the issues of evangelism and conversion. Yet in choosing a fixed position the authors appear to turn away from their insistence that our appreciation of *what gurus do* must be rooted in empirical observation. Thus Greatbatch and Clark (2005) observe that 'the notion that gurus are powerful evangelical actors is central to the existing literature' (24). Yet they insist that this representation of the guru seminar as a process of evangelical 'conversion' led by an evangelist offers only a 'caricature', albeit one which 'dominates present understandings', and so goes 'unquestioned' (21). Challenging this 'caricature', however, Greatbatch and Clark appear to turn from the nuanced and data-led discussion that shaped their earlier paper (Clark and Greatbatch, 2002). Thus the authors suggest that 'management guru lectures have more in common with those that take place in university lecture theatres or at organizational conferences' (24). Yet Greatbatch and Clark (2005) fail to account for this blanket assertion and make no attempt to ground it within an empirical frame. This omission produces a small catalogue of questions and issues which deserve, I suggest, further consideration:

- Why is it categorically incorrect to suggest that guru seminars are akin to conversion events?
- Was Tom Peters accurately portrayed as an evangelist seeking converts in 2002? And if so had he, by 2005, turned his back upon the evangelical approach that most observers suggest is central to his approach and persona?
- In what ways would a university lecture mirror the performance dynamics of a guru seminar? And what steps have the authors taken to validate this assertion?

I do not intend to respond to these questions on a case-by-case basis. They are, after all, largely rhetorical in nature! That said, it is worth observing that in other renderings of their research Clark and Greatbatch do provide responses to at least some of the issues raised here. Unfortunately, the responses offered appear to contradict the statements reproduced above insofar as they suggest that guru seminars do, in fact, amount to conversion experiences. Thus Greatbatch and Clark (2003: 1539) assert that guru performances *are* events that 'create the conditions necessary to win and retain converts'. Furthermore, it is worth observing that in a later paper, Clark, this time working with others (see Groβ et al., 2015: 275), reproduces this section of text, adding the qualification that such events 'are critical' (275) to the process whereby new disciples are won. Ten years on from the production of *Management Speak* (Greatbatch and Clark, 2005), therefore, Clark appears to signal that he is, despite his earlier public statements, now fully converted to an evangelical conceptualisation of the guru performer!

Yet confusion reigns. Clark and Greatbatch (2002) observe that guru performers build and depend upon stories to 'establish the voracity and legitimacy of the ideas that they are communicating' (161). Accounting for the use of stories within this context, however, the authors argue that gurus are obliged to fall back upon storytelling because, unlike their counterparts in the universities, they 'lack a formal and authoritative body of knowledge' (Clark and Greatbatch, 2002: 161) that might justify their essential truth claims.

These contradictory assertions suggest that the texts which provide the very foundations for research into 'guru speak' proceed in the absence of a stable conceptualisation of the guru-performer and are, despite the attacks which Clark and Greatbatch launch upon their contemporaries, largely *a priori* and consequently not grounded within an empirical frame.[4] In chapter six we will attempt to provide a stable conceptualisation of management's gurus which, in being founded upon a clear-headed and explicitly rendered conceptualisation of the guru-as-performer, can support useful academic inquiry. Before we can do this, however, we must pause to consider the methodology that underpins 'guru speak'.

The methodology of guru speak

Greatbatch and Clark (2005) argue that any attempt to account for the practice of 'guru speak' must recognise the manner in which guru seminars differ from the textual sources that are typically examined when guru theorising is subject to academic scrutiny. Reflecting upon these seminar events, Greatbatch and Clark point out that the speakers in this context are expected, not only to inform, but to engage and to entertain those present. Teasing out the implications of this observation, they note that guru seminars are, intrinsically, precarious events because the man, or woman, before the lectern remains always dependent – visibly and viscerally – upon the continuing enrolment of the audience. Recognising this need for enrolment, Greatbatch and Clark (2005) argue that stories offer the 'key to understanding how [gurus] gain reputations as powerful orators' (33). Consequently, much of the work developed by the authors (see Clark and Greatbatch, 2002; Greatbatch and Clark, 2003, 2005) has been devoted to an analysis of the tales that gurus employ in their seminar events. Yet as they analyse the tales rendered by their gurus, Clark and Greatbatch (2002: 156) mount a challenge to, what they term, the 'elaborate' and 'terse' approaches to storytelling.

Elaborate and terse approaches to storytelling

The 'elaborate' account of storytelling is, for students of organisation, perhaps most closely associated with the work of Gabriel (2000; see also Collins, 2018). Gabriel argues that poetic or proper stories are special forms of narrative which possess core structural characteristics. Taking his cue from Aristotle, therefore, Gabriel suggests that stories:

•   Involve characters in a predicament.
•   Unfold according to a chain of events that reflects a) the structure of the plot and b) the essential traits of the characters involved.

- Call upon symbolism/symbolic matters.
- Indulge poetic embellishment and narrative development.
- Have an arc which moves the reader/audience from a beginning through a middle section to a successful conclusion.
- Seek a connection not with simple facts but with local understandings and/or more general truths.

Boje's (1991, 2001) 'terse' alternative to the 'elaborate' narratives preferred by Gabriel captures many of the points detailed here. Furthermore, Boje's analysis of storytelling practices usefully highlights the interactions and the interruptions that so often intrude upon attempts to render a story for an audience that is physically present.

Accounting for the presence of storytelling in our everyday lives, Boje takes his cue from Weick (1995). He observes that, on a day-to-day basis, each of us confronts a key problem: how to make sense of a 'complex soup' of ambiguous and half-understood problems, events and experiences. Reflecting upon this problem of ambiguity, Boje suggests that people are obliged to construct and retrace their lives, retrospectively, through stories. He warns us, however, that we must distinguish 'stories' from 'narratives' if we are fully to understand the richness of organisational sensemaking. Narratives are, he warns, plotted, directed and staged to produce a linear, coherent and monological rendering of events, while 'stories are self-deconstructing, flowing, emerging and networking, not at all static' (Boje, 2001: 1).

Elaborating on the need to distinguish 'narratives' from 'stories', Boje (2001: 9) complains that 'so much of what passes for academic narrative analysis in organization studies seems to rely upon sequential, single-voiced stories'. In an attempt to provide an alternative to these monologues of business endeavour, he introduces the concept of the 'antenarrative'.

For Boje (2001), 'antenarrative' has two faces. On one face, Boje's focus upon 'antenarrative' is based upon the assertion that 'stories' precede 'narrative'. Thus Boje suggests that stories are 'antenarrative' insofar as they come before the processes of staging and directing, which, as he sees it, lead to the development of 'sequential, single-voiced', top-down 'narratives'. On the obverse face, Boje calls upon the rules of poker and suggests that an 'antenarrative' represents 'a bet' (or 'an ante') that retrospective sensemaking may emerge in the future from 'the fragmented, non-linear, incoherent, collective and unplotted' (2001: 1) stories, which come before corporate monologues.

This 'antenarrative' approach overlaps to some degree with the account offered by Gabriel (2000). In common with Boje, Gabriel observes that stories offer local and intimate accounts of situations, events and predicaments. Indeed, reflecting upon the complexities associated with the analysis of stories and storytelling, Gabriel argues that 'storywork' – literally the art of constructing meaningful stories – is a delicately woven product of intimate knowledge. Furthermore, Gabriel concurs with Boje that it is vitally important to distinguish 'stories' from other 'narrative' forms. Yet at this point the accounts of storytelling prepared by Boje and Gabriel diverge quite fundamentally.

Commenting upon the craft of storytelling, both Boje and Gabriel have complained that it can be difficult to unearth good stories and talented storytellers in organisations. Indeed, each has suggested that it is becoming increasingly difficult to witness organisational storytelling in its naturally intimate surroundings. This shared recognition of poetic decline, however, takes Boje and Gabriel in opposite analytical directions.

Lamenting the perceived decline in organisational stories, Gabriel (2000) simply renews his commitment to the understanding that stories are (increasingly rare and) special forms of narrative with definite characteristics. Boje, however, adopts a rather different approach which seeks to redefine the very nature of organisational stories. In an initial move, Boje (1991) suggests a 'terse' approach. Thus he suggests that within the conversational give-and-take of storytelling *in situ*, the four words which announce 'you know the story' is actually equivalent to telling a poetic tale. Later, in a more radical move, Boje (2001) suggests an 'antenarrative' account which, as we have seen, suggests that stories should be regarded as those special forms of narrative that exist *prior* to the crystallising processes of casting and plotting. Gabriel, however, disputes these assertions.

For Gabriel, stories – despite literary deskilling – represent a rich and, in any sense, a vital resource for organisational theorists. And on this matter he and Boje are in perfect agreement: Stories are interesting because they allow us to experience the dynamic flow that is social organisation. But for Gabriel plots, staging and direction constitute the central characteristics of stories. Taking issue with Boje, therefore, Gabriel protests that while the so-called 'terse stories' observed by his contemporary represent invitations to recall either a pattern of events or a particular rendering of a tale, they are not, properly-speaking, stories. Similar concerns apply to Boje's (2001) antenarrative conceptualisation of organisational stories.

Boje's suspicion of narrative monologues, as we have seen, stems from a concern that academics and business commentators have been, altogether, too keen to endorse a sensegiving account of storytelling (see Gioia and Chittipeddi, 1991) and have, as a consequence, colonised the organisational world with tales that are linear, single-voiced and top-down in their orientation. Noting both the practical consequences and the analytical limitations of such sensegiving accounts of storytelling, Boje (2001) suggests that we should be suspicious of corporate plotting and should, in an attempt to free ourselves from such hegemonies, embrace 'antenarratives' which, as the name suggests, come before the crystallising processes of plot formation. Collins (2007, 2018), however, suggests that Boje's (2001) 'antenarrative' account fails because it rejects and yet depends upon plotting and characterisation. Indeed, Boje's (2001) 'antenarrative' tales breach the covenant formed between the storyteller and her audience.

Reflecting upon the stories rendered by the gurus, Clark and Greatbatch (2002) review the 'elaborate' account advanced by Gabriel (2000) and the 'terse' model advanced by Boje (1991) and reject both. They suggest that neither the 'elaborate' structural account preferred by Gabriel (2000) nor the 'terse' approach preferred by Boje (1991, 2001) offer a useful appreciation of storytelling *in situ*. Advancing their preferred alternative, they counter that their 'approach is not to conceive of a story as a performed entity which is transmitted by a storyteller but rather as a performative activity whose emergent character is dependent upon in situ behaviours of the participants and whose meanings may vary across contexts' (155). Building upon this account of audience dynamics, Greatbatch and Clark assert that both the 'elaborate' and the 'terse' approach to storytelling are flawed because they proceed from an account of storytelling that is structural in character, and so, predicated upon 'a priori formal definitions' (110) of narrative form.

Countering this structural approach, Greatbatch and Clark (2005) insist that stories must be defined, not by narrative form, but by public proclamation. Stressing the importance of this bugle call, the authors tell us that:

> The gurus have to indicate that they are about to tell a story so that the members of the audience hear what is being presented as a story.
>
> (110)

Recognising the extent to which the storyteller is dependent upon audience affiliation, however, they are immediately obliged to qualify this statement. Thus Greatbatch and Clark (2005) add that any segment of talk, which is announced as a tale must also be 'recognizable and hearable as a story' (110).

But if stories are defined in the social space that remains between the speaker's proclamation and the audience's reaction, how can Greatbatch and Clark be sure that what the gurus choose to announce as 'stories' have, in fact, been recognised and heard by the congregation in these terms?

The short answer is that the authors cannot, and choose simply to ignore this issue. Greatbatch and Clark therefore blithely assume that they know a) what the audience can hear, b) what the audience can recognise and c) what the audience will choose to define as a story. Thus the bald assertion that 'Peters told 12 stories' (Greatbatch and Clark, 2005: 112) in the seminar performance(s) reviewed makes sense *only* if we accept that Greatbatch and Clark can know in advance what an audience might find 'hearable' as a story. Yet the authors rule out this presumption. Indeed they insist that any attempt to define stories *a priori* and in relation to their narrative form would be high-handed and deterministic.

This account of storytelling places a very serious contradiction at the heart of the project advanced by Clark and Greatbatch. Thus Greatbatch and Clark (2005) insist that their preferred analytical approach has been developed to enable us to explore the manner in which gurus structure their speech to secure the enrolment and ongoing agreement of their audiences. And yet the authors' desire to generate a radical restatement on the very nature of stories actively prevents the realisation of this agenda because it prevents the development of a robust methodology that can examine and account for their core concerns.

In our next section we will expand upon this issue as we consider the 'findings' which build and depend upon this failed methodology.

Analysing the practice of storytelling

As we commence this section it is appropriate that we pause again to acknowledge that, together, Greatbatch and Clark have generated an outline agenda for academic inquiry that is novel, distinctive and, yes, insightful. Indeed, we should acknowledge that the authors' analyses do highlight the important role which stories perform in guru theorising. Thus Greatbatch and Clark suggest that their gurus use stories:

- To establish their status as members of an organisational elite that enjoys privileged access to those who manage and control the world's most notable corporations.
- To attack contemporary organisational practices in a manner that insulates the audience present from culpability for such failings.
- To keep the audience interested. Indeed, Clark and Greatbatch (2002: 166) suggest that stories are, within the context of the guru performance, 'distinct units of talk'; 'islands of vocal interaction in an otherwise silently received performance' which punctuate presentations in a pleasing manner.
- To secure and manage the enrolment of the audience in their project. In this regard it is worth noting that Clark and Greatbatch (2002: 166) observe that stories should be regarded as 'distinct units of talk' within which 'gurus and audience members are most often engaged directly with one another'.

Yet to endorse these findings as robust and reliable, we must be prepared to accept that Clark and Greatbatch have a methodology that can, reliably, discriminate between general speech and those special forms of narrative that qualify as stories. And this is, as we have seen, and as we will consider later, very much open to question.

In what follows we will suggest that the empirical claims advanced by the authors are over-stated: At best they require qualification and/or further contextualisation and at worst they are simply unsupported by the data. To advance this line of analysis, we will focus predominantly on Greatbatch and Clark (2005) since this text offers the largest and the most elaborate account of guru performance advanced by the authors. We begin by placing the claims advanced by the authors within an account of their data-set.

Data concerns and characteristics

Greatbatch and Clark (2005) offer an analysis of the seminar performances offered by their four gurus. They observe that the gurus employ similar rhetorical techniques, yet exhibit differences in speaking style. This is a perfectly plausible finding. Yet in accounting for the conduct of the gurus they observe, the authors too often fail to acknowledge the limitations inherent in both their methodology and their data-set. In short, they place exclamation marks in their text at those points where question marks are, in fact, merited.[5]

Analysing extracts of but one pre-recorded lecture, for example, Greatbatch and Clark report that Hamel expects his audience to remain attentive yet passive. Contrasting this presentational style with the other gurus in their study, Greatbatch and Clark observe that Peters, Senge and Kanter seek a more interactive relationship with their audiences. Indeed, they observe that Peters is wont to hector audience members and will *routinely* fix audience members in his gaze as he attempts to communicate key points.

Commenting upon the approach adopted by Peter Senge, Greatbatch and Clark (2005) suggest that this guru's presentational style is unique: 'only Senge invites audiences to respond to questions either verbally or non-verbally (by raising their hands)' (38). This is an intriguing observation. But it cannot constitute a generalisable truth-claim. And it is too easily falsified.

For example, in a seminar delivered at The Brewery, London on March 17, 2005,[6] Tom Peters poses *direct* questions to and solicits responses from his audience on a number of occasions. I offer but one example:

The Brewery (disc two) 00:16:25[7]

How many of you=I hope the answer is not zero=have ever seen a Cirque de Soleil Performance? (10).

A lot of you.

Shouldn't the finance department be like a Cirque de Soleil Performance? L-L-L

No I'm serious. It's about excellence isn't it?=It's about amazing things you just couldn't imagine until you saw.

In addition, it is worth pointing out that in a seminar delivered in the Peacock Theatre some four years later in London on September 3, 2009, Tom Peters[8] invites his audience to respond to direct questions no fewer than four times. Indeed, he invites and, where necessary, cajoles the audience to respond to his questions three times within the first 23 minutes of his seminar presentation. Again, a single example is sufficient to illustrate the point:

Peacock Theatre 00:22:54

How long is it after the patient begins to talk before the doctor interrupts him? (20)
    So that was not a rhetorical question. Tell me what the hell the answer is. I'm listening.

Anthony Robbins, a guru known to encourage his followers to engage in 'fire-walking' as a means of overcoming the self-doubt that prevents (as he sees it) the realisation of their full potential, also poses questions to and invites a response from his audience. Indeed, it may be useful to observe that in the recording detailed here, Robbins appears to take this Q and A to a level unimagined by Greatbatch and Clark. Thus in the *Unlimited Power* seminar[9] (published in 1986), Anthony Robbins does something that is, we are told, unique to Senge's preferred approach: He asks direct questions of his audience. Furthermore, it is plain that the audience present, unlike that gathered before Tom Peters, does not immediately assume that the speaker's questioning is rhetorical in nature.

Unlimited Power

Audio-tape (side one) 00.03.00

This is a communications seminar (5) Aahh (5) tricked you.
    If I would have said this is a communications seminar how many of you would have shown up?
    [speaker may be heard laughing]
    Ah (5) that's what I was afraid of.
    L-L-L
    Two instead of three hundred. OK.
    The reason it's a communications seminar is because I believe communication is the key to your life. In fact you might want to start your notes with the following phrase: This is what this seminar is all about.
    Write down: (5) The quality of my life (5) is the quality of my communication (10).
    The quality of my life i:s the quality of my personal communication. Here's what I mean by this (5).

In order to have any quality of life you have to communicate with who? (10)

Yourself.

You see the quality of your life is how you communicate with yourself.

How many of you have ever had a relationship with someone in your life who maybe left you?

Did any of you ever have that experience?

Anybody here?

Ok.

In the second extract reproduced below we rejoin the *Unlimited Power* seminar just a few moments after our first extract concludes. In this extract we, again, hear Robbins asking questions, but this time he is more directive and makes clear the nature of the response which he requires.

Unlimited Power

Audio-tape (side one) 00.04.30

How many of you here would like to make a major difference to the world?

Can I see a show of hands? (20)

How many of you would like to lie on the beach and get tanned?

[speaker may be heard laughing]

L-L-L

Does that cause a problem sometimes?

[speaker may be heard laughing]

Our third extract is the briefest of those reproduced. It is, however, the most interesting because it suggests that the audiences has 'warmed up' and is now willing to respond audibly and collectively to the questioning that has characterised the opening few minutes of the seminar.

Unlimited Power

Audio-tape (side one) 16:10

Is energy all you need to succeed?

[Audience] *No:o*

Of course I cannot be sure that Tom Peters' conduct at these events is typical. Nor would I assert that the behaviour of Anthony Robbins is, in the extracts I have reproduced, actually characteristic of his style and conduct – although

I suspect it may well be. What may be said with confidence, however, is that there is ample evidence to suggest that in their seminar presentations, Tom Peters and Anthony Robbins have actively invited the verbal and non-verbal participation of their audiences and on that basis we can refute what appears to be the generalised assertion that Senge's approach is 'unique'.

We will now look in more detail at the claims which Greatbatch and Clark (2005) make as to the storytelling practices evident from their observations of the gurus.

Telling tales

Clark and Greatbatch (2002) observe that both Tom Peters and Rosabeth Moss Kanter each tell at least one tale, which indulges a form of 'flexing'. That is to say that each renders a tale which serves to highlight their presence at the very pinnacle of our most prestigious business organisations. Beyond this shared common practice, however, the authors also highlight important differences in approach, which they tell us serve to distinguish the performances offered by Peters and by Kanter.

Kanter, they suggest, is inclined to render tales which place her as an academic consultant working with organisations whereas Peters is, they observe, more inclined to render tales that deal with his day-to-day experiences and frustrations as a paying customer. Having attended seminars by both speakers, I have no reason to doubt this observation. Yet I also suggest that this bald observation deserves further reflection, consideration and contextualisation.

Clark and Greatbatch, as we have seen, complain that academic attempts to come to terms with the gurus have, in effect, removed the central actor – the guru – from the analytical frame. This is, I accept, a fair assessment of the field. Yet in seeking to place the guru front and centre, Clark and Greatbatch appear to have developed a curiously truncated, timeless and decontextualised account of their gurus which effectively denies these actors a career and a biography. Thus the suggestion that Peters builds his seminar around tales of consumption and the frustrations thereof, I suggest, needs now to be (re)framed, contingently, as being reflective of a particular phase of the career of Tom Peters. In this regard, it may be helpful to note that Collins (2007) has offered a critical review and analysis of the stories that Peters has published in his key texts. This research suggests that this guru's published tales of shopping and consumer dissatisfaction appear at a later stage of his career. Far from being an inherent component of the speaker's style and approach, therefore, Tom Peters' consumer tales actually signal his withdrawal from those organisational connections that, at the start of his career, delivered him to global notoriety. Let us turn now to consider the manner in which the gurus announce their stories.

Greatbatch and Clark (2005) observe that the four speakers who constitute their research sample mark the 'islands of vocal interaction' (Clark and
Greatbatch, 2002: 166) that signal the advent of a story by using prefacing
devices. These prefacing devices are, they add, remarkably similar. Thus
the authors tell us that the gurus announce their tales either implicitly – 'A
while back, a year roughly' (113) – or explicitly – 'this is sort of one of my
favourite stories' (112).

Accounting for this practice, Greatbatch and Clark (2005) suggest that
such prefacing devices are important in the context of lengthy seminar presentations because they act to punctuate the event and, in so doing, 'increase
the listenability of the next segment of talk by a) highlighting their content
from surrounding speech materials and b) projecting a clear point from the
onset of the story in question' (116).

Leaving aside the methodological difficulties, which undermine the ability of the authors to frame segments of talk as stories, we should concede
that this is a perfectly sensible argument in the context of a classical or
'elaborate' account of storytelling. Speakers who punctuate their addresses
with pithy observations and comic asides are generally more welcome than
those who simply drone on and on. Yet we may extend this analysis to take
fuller account of the audience present.

In preceding paragraphs we suggested that there is a need to allow the
gurus a biography as we account for the utterances, which structure and
convey guru presentations. Here we will suggest that there is also a need
to allow the audience a biography. This enriched appreciation of the audience, its needs and its identity, I suggest, demands that we should be prepared
to countenance the possibility of alternative and/or supplementary forms
of explanation that can account for the use of the story prefaces which
Greatbatch and Clark have observed.[10] For example, repeated use of a story
preface that alludes to the privileged status of a particular tale might be
interpreted as the speaker seeking a licence to relay a section of talk that
a significant proportion of the audience may well have encountered previously, in print or at a prior seminar.

Equally, usage of the 'favourite story' preface might be interpreted as
an utterance directed to those such as booking agents, newspaper editors
and publishers who are, of course, vital to the gurus' marketability (see
Davenport et al., 2003). In this context the 'favourite story' preface might
be viewed as doing (at least) two things. Firstly – as we noted earlier – it
acts to make a legitimate space for a tale that may be familiar to sections
of the audience. Secondly, as Clark and Greatbatch (2002) acknowledge,
it suggests that the speaker has chosen carefully from a large repertoire of
tales which, in being products of experience, act as an index of authority. We
could, however, extend this discussion yet further.

In common with Greatbatch and Clark (2005), Westwood (2007) observes that performance is a fragile process. Indeed, he insists that performers are vulnerable and must take steps to project an appropriate identity whenever they stand before an audience. This recognition of the performer's vulnerability, and of the active co-production of performance, makes space for the suggestion that the story prefacing device observed by Greatbatch and Clark might now be investigated as the means by which the speaker punctuates the performance *for their own benefit*. This suggestion, we would do well to note, arises from initial inquires conducted with 'public speakers' – in a variety of guises. These preliminary inquiries suggest that those who speak in public, but who are generally denied access to either a script or detailed notes (such as comedians), often construct their performances around a number of fairly stable segments of speech or 'routines'. Furthermore, initial inquiries with such speakers suggest that, as they mentally divide their presentational work into a number of distinct segments, they condense and curate these into but one or two memorable phrases. Such words and phrases, I suggest, effectively constitute a mental map of the performance event. Given this mapping practice, there is, I propose, room for the suggestion that we might now explore the extent to which the 'favourite story' preface constitutes a navigation device; a 'way marker' erected for the speaker's benefit, which allows him/her a) to manage the anxieties inherent in every performance while b) delivering a performance experience that is fluent, fluid and so pleasing for all present. In the context of an enlarged performance dynamic, therefore, the prefacing device observed by Greatbatch and Clark might now be investigated as a mechanism that allows the speaker to mark and to move between the various elements, or utterances, that constitute the seminar performance as a whole.

Yet no matter how we choose to rationalise this prefacing device, we should not assume that reference to a preferred, or favourite, anecdote means that the guru in question intends simply to retell his/her story. As our next chapter will make plain, audiences appreciate presentations that are well-constructed and speakers who are fluent and well-rehearsed. They resent however those performers who merely 'go through the motions'. In pursuit of this appreciation of the dynamics of live performance, chapter six will commence with reflections on 'performance theory' as a prelude to a consideration of the nature and dynamics of stand-up comedy. This account of stand-up comedy, we will suggest, offers an opportunity *and* the means to reframe our understanding of *what gurus do*.

Concluding comments

This chapter has offered a critical, analytical review of the attempts that Clark and Greatbatch have made to understand guru performances. We have acknowledged the discontents that underpin this project. Indeed we have accepted that, for the most part, the critique developed by Clark and Greatbatch is fair and accurate. In short, we have acknowledged that Clark and Greatbatch are pioneers in this arena. Yet we have suggested that, as pioneers tend to, Clark and Greatbatch have driven their horses further and harder than is truly merited.[11] Or more plainly, we have argued that the 'guru speak' project – the attempt to locate, understand and account for the performances which the gurus develop through their seminars – is undermined by problems conceptual, methodological and empirical. Reflecting upon these issues, we have argued that the 'guru speak' project, despite its desire to develop an empirically-informed appreciation of guru performance, proceeds in the absence of a stable conceptualisation of the guru performer that might enable this aspiration.

We have also observed the authors' desire to develop a critical restatement of the nature of stories. We have argued that this notionally audience-centred account of stories is, however, unnecessary and unhelpful. It is unnecessary because Gabriel's (2000) structural or 'elaborate' account of stories and storytelling may easily accommodate an audience and can readily incorporate their interactions with the speaker. It is unhelpful because it denies the authors access to a methodology that can appreciate the dynamics of storytelling in this context.

Finally, we have offered reflections on the empirical observations voiced by the authors. We have argued that the bald claims made as to the performance styles and approaches of the gurus are over-stated and too easily falsified. Furthermore, we have argued that Greatbatch and Clark tend to treat guru performances in isolation, and so deny both speaker and audience a biography that might contextualise and/or explain the dynamics observed. In our next chapter we will attempt to build upon the intuitions of Greatbatch and Clark in a fashion that overcomes the limits in execution revealed by our analysis. Chapter six will suggest, therefore, that we might come to a fuller appreciation of the nature and processes of guru performance if we are willing to frame this within an account of the performance art that goes by the name of stand-up comedy.

Notes

1 Actually, Clark and Greatbatch (2002) suggest that the gurus face two challenges. To assist understanding, I have chosen to sub-divide the second component highlighted by the authors. I suggest therefore that it is useful to highlight three, albeit overlapping, issues.

2 Greatbatch and Clark (2005) suggest that there are just two works that offer sustained analyses of guru performance. These are the texts produced by Sharpe (1984) and Oliver (1998). In an earlier paper, however, Greatbatch and Clark (2003) highlight the existence of *three* prior studies of performance by adding the work of Guerrier and Gilbert (1995).

3 This is, of course, a misreading of Lewin's analysis. Readers may wish to consult Burnes (2004).

4 It is perhaps worth observing that in the social sciences, suggestions of 'determinism' generally constitute a very grave insult!

5 This is, of course, a reference to the dossier on Iraq's ability to launch 'weapons of mass destruction' developed by Tony Blair's UK government and the subsequent inquiry which suggested that the case for intervention had been very much exaggerated.

6 A full recording of this event is available from Red Audio. The event was organised by the London Business Forum.

7 I employ the transcription notation developed by Atkinson and Heritage (1994). The numbers reproduced above each textual extract signal in hours, minutes and seconds the position that the segment of talk occupies in the overall performance. Where the performance has been recorded onto a number of components, the disc number is listed. The following conventions are employed in the transcripts reproduced in this chapter:

(5)   Numbers in parentheses indicate the length of a period of silence. This is calculated in tenths of a second.

Word Underlining indicates that the word has been stressed by the speaker.
Wo:rd Colons rendered thus indicate that the sound preceding has been prolonged.
L-L-L This is used to indicate spasmodic laughter.
= This is used to denote overlapping speech.

8 This seminar was organised by the London Business Forum. A full recording of the event is available from Red Audio.

9 An audio-tape recording produced by Audioworks (a division of Simon and Schuster) is available to purchase.

10 Groß et al. (2015) undertake an element of this work as they consider the motivations of audience members present at guru seminars. In the absence of further information concerning the identities of the speakers involved in this study, however, questions remain as to the extent to which those whom the authors label as gurus can meaningfully lay claim to this status.

11 I am sure that I owe this allusion to a scholar from a previous generation, although I do wish that it was my own! I have made strenuous efforts to find the source so that I might give due credit. Thus far, I have failed in my efforts.

6 Reframing guru performance

Introduction

In chapter five we offered a critical, analytical review of the account of guru performance developed collectively by Clark and Greatbatch (2002, 2003; Greatbatch and Clark, 2003, 2005). We conceded that the authors' desire to generate an appreciation of guru performance, *in situ*, has generated an account of 'guru speak' that recognises and responds to the limitations associated with current academic practice in this arena. And yet we have argued that the 'guru speak' project has been damaged by conceptual, methodological and empirical failings which undermine its core intent. Chapter five concluded, therefore, with the suggestion that guru performance truly merits further inquiry but will need to be reframed if such research is to be worthwhile.

In this chapter we offer an alternative frame for future research in this arena. We will suggest that we should now work to explore the extent to which the guru-performer might usefully be located with an account of the performance processes and practices which constitute stand-up comedy. This chapter *will not* suggest that management's gurus are simply stand-up comics, nor will it suggest that guru performance exists as a sub-set of stand-up comedy. It will, however, argue that the failure to develop a stable and empirically-grounded understanding of the guru-as-performer seriously limits the 'guru speak' project such that that we should now consider a new conceptualisation of the guru-performer. To this end our chapter is structured as follows.

We begin with reflections upon 'performance'. Clark and Greatbatch, it is plain, understand that their gurus are, at root, performers. Yet their research tends to produce a de-contextualised account of the performers, their performances and indeed their audiences. In an attempt to develop a fuller appreciation of 'guru speak', which can acknowledge these dimensions, we commence with an account of Schechner's ([1977] 2003) now classic analysis. This text, as we shall see, moves 'performance' from its elevated position on-stage back into everyday life. In addition, Schechner's analysis reminds us that successful performance, wherever it is enacted (lecture-room, boardroom . . . bedroom), requires each of us to construct and to maintain a mask – a performed biography.

Having considered Schechner's analysis, the third section will offer reflections on stand-up comedy. This performance activity, while familiar, is rather difficult to define. This is, of course, problematic at one level. Academia is naturally drawn to categorisations that are neat and clearly delineated. That is why organisational behaviour texts are weighed down by 2x2 matrices!

Yet we will argue that the variety evident within stand-up comedy is potentially productive for it demands that we acknowledge something which Clark and Greatbatch (2002) initially conceded and then either forgot or rejected: that 'guru performers' exhibit complex and contrasting styles which merit explanation. Recognising this, we will argue that reframing the dynamics of guru-performance within an account of stand-up comedy has the capacity to advance academic understanding insofar as it demands that we explain and account for:

1 The conduct of individual gurus *in situ*.
2 Audience enrolment before, during and after the event.
3 The stories which the gurus use to generate and precipitate audience affiliation.
4 The choices available to the gurus as they construct and render their tales.
5 The nature of the performed biographies which the gurus construct in their attempts to ensure that their on-stage projections are accepted as being, accurate, productive and authentic.

In pursuit of these elements we will signal key themes, which we suggest might now usefully underpin a reframed research agenda on guru perfor-mance. Thus we will consider the manner in which an analysis of:

- 'identity-work'
- 'disclosure'
- 'liveness'
- 'repair' and finally

might be used to reframe and in so doing to enhance academic understand-ing of guru performance.

Placing performance in everyday life

In his now classic treatment of the subject, Schechner ([1977] 2003) offers a distinctive appreciation of the nature of performance. Building upon Goffman's (1959) work, Schechner tells us that performance is a feature of everyday life and is to be found in 'play, games, sports, theatre and ritual' (8). Examining the shared attributes which unite these apparently separate events, Schechner highlights four key dimensions of performance.

Firstly he observes that performance involves us in gatherings which have special methods of ordering time. These methods may focus upon 'event time' when, for example, 'the activity, itself, has a set sequence that must be completed no matter how long (or short) the elapsed clock time' (8); 'set time', 'where an arbitrary time pattern is imposed on events' (8), for example the 12 rounds of three-minute duration commonly associated with professional boxing; and 'symbolic time', as may be present in 'make-believe play and games' (8).

Secondly Schechner argues that performance events, however they are constituted in time, often attach a special value to objects, even where they have little intrinsic or monetary worth. These special objects may be props in theatrical and/or film productions. Such objects might include, for example, 'the Ring' in *The Lord of the Rings* stories. Off-stage, special objects might include the finishing tape in a foot race and the try-line in rugby football.

Thirdly Schechner reminds us that within a world where 'time is money', performance events revel in their non-productivity. It is, in short, enough for a performance to be beautiful, funny or simply moving.

Fourth and finally, Schechner points out that performance events have rules, which tell those involved in the 'performance' what they may do and *vice versa*. These rules, he is careful to point out, are co-constructed over time. Acknowledging the significance of this inner world of performance and the connection, however mediated, with the outside world, Schechner suggests that performance is bounded at its outer limit, or frame, by some notion of *space* and moves through layers of *convention, drama* and *direction* until an inner *free* zone is reached. Accounting for the presence of this free zone at the very core of the performance event, Schechner reminds us that the actor on the theatrical stage may, in the moment, choose to deviate from the script and/or the staging demanded by the director. Equally, the defensive midfielder on the football pitch may ignore the instructions of his coach and, in so doing, allow the opposing striker to evade the offside trap. This latter observation, we should note, suggests that there are risks associated with the exercise of such freedoms.

Noting that apparently separate and distinctive performance events involve 'gathering', 'performing' and 'dispersing', Schechner highlights the significance of 'routine' (structures, calendars, places and symbols) and 'routines' (segments of speech and action which in being readily available to the performer may be said to constitute a repertoire). Teasing out the significance of 'the socio-theatrical conventions' (x) which underpin the repertoires that frame performance genres, Schechner highlights the presence of a discourse community which, because it must agree to the performance *and* retain the power to object to its elaboration, must be enrolled by the performer(s). Discussing the manner in which such constraints impinge upon the performers' choices and the associated scope for action, Schechner draws our attention to the identity-work at the heart of performance: Personae, he tells us, need to be 'devised' (x) if the performer's routine is to be successful!

Schechner's analysis makes it plain therefore that performance, wherever it is enacted, remains an emotional, complex and regulated process. Nonetheless, he makes it plain that performance contains degrees of freedom and, with the indulgence of the audience, may be carried off in a variety of ways. In the following section we will place these general reflections upon 'performance' within the context of stand-up comedy.

Stand-up comedy

Double's (2005) 'standard definition' (Butler and Stoyanova Russell, 2018: 7) of stand-up comedy is often used to introduce this form of performance art. This definition (so-called) suggests that a stand-up comedian is a 'single performer standing in front of an audience, talking to them directly with the specific intention of making them laugh' (Double, 2005: 4). The problem, of course, is that this general (so-called) definition is bland, narrowly descriptive and, consequently, largely uninformative. It is, in addition, potentially misleading because as Butler and Stoyanova-Russell (2018: 7) note, stand-up comedy 'may also involve musical acts, double acts and sketch troupes'. Mintz's (1985: 71) definition of stand-up comedy is even more inclusive. He concedes that a 'strict definition of standup comedy would describe an encounter between a single, standing performer behaving comically and/or saying funny things directly to an audience unsupported by very much in the way of costume, prop setting or dramatic vehicle'. And yet he observes that stand-up comedy has roots in 'rites, rituals and dramatic experiences that are richer . . . than this simple definition can embrace'. Consequently, Mintz suggests that a more useful account of stand-up comedy, while stressing the directness of the artist/audience communication, would 'include seated story-tellers [and], comic characterizations that employ costume and prop [and] team acts' (71).

Attempts to trace the lineage of stand-up comedy generally concede that it has, however we choose to define the performer(s), a complex history. As

Brodie's (2008) observations imply, stand-up comedy may be traced back to the 'Victorian music hall and early 20th-century variety theatre, as well as earlier European traditions of minstrels and jesters' (Butler and Stoyanova-Russell, 2018: 7). Most histories of stand-up comedy, while tracing and accepting this lineage, however, also suggest an evolutionary break some-time around the late 1970s or early 1980s. During this period, it is suggested a new breed of 'alternative comedians' emerged. These performers, we are assured, were less inclined to build their acts upon (racist and sexist) jokes and instead chose to locate their humour within political reflection and, more generally, upon observations derived (apparently) from their day-to-day experience. De La Tour (2013; see also Kind, 2011), however, suggests that such potted histories, while commonly accepted and repeated, tend to romanticise the stand-up comedian and indeed the whole 'scene'. Thus De La Tour argues that the supposed presence of a new stand-up comedy, based upon a rejection of previous standards and mores, fails to acknowledge the extent to which acts which indulge and project racism, misogyny and anti-Islamic sentiments, for example, continue to attract paying customers.

Brodie (2008) adds a technological component to the discussion of stand-up comedy. He suggests that the development of microphone technology has been central to the development of what most commentators would now take to be the central characteristic of stand-up comedy. Thus Brodie sug-gests that the development of microphone technology has facilitated the movement *from* merely cracking jokes *to* the performance of extended nar-ratives with nested humorous elements. Noting the manner in which the per-formances developed by contemporary stand-up comedians contrasts with the humourists who plied their trade on the music hall stage, Brodie argues that it is the voice-amplification made possible by microphone technology which has facilitated the development of the prolonged and intimate story-telling performance (denied to the earlier music-hall performer) that is now characteristic of stand-up comedy.

Despite the tendency to romanticise the history of stand-up, there is, I suggest, a skeletal appreciation of this form of performance that we might use to shape both our appreciation of stand-up comedy and future research on *what gurus say*. I suggest, therefore, that stand-up comics depend upon the continuing enrolment and affiliation of their audiences. And like the gurus, stand-up comedians (1) nest their concerns within projections which have both a humorous intent and (often) a more serious message – even if the message is, as Schechner insists, that we are always on-stage and under scrutiny by others. Yet, whatever the 'true' function of the voiced projec-tions of the stand-up comedian, it is plain that these build (2) upon extended narratives that call upon (3) stories and (4) broader observations and asides to secure (5) an identity which in being (6) plausibly authentic develops (7) a world-view and through this a shared point-of-view that (8) causes laughter. In what follows, we will examine the manner in which 'identity-work', 'disclosure', 'liveness', 'repair' and 'authenticity' allow us to place some flesh on this skeleton.

Identity-work

Schechner ([1977] 2003), as we have seen, argues that performers must variously adopt or construct personae to make their contributions plausible. Commenting upon his very public, if faltering, gestation as a sports commentator, Boulting (2011), for example, makes it plain that even those who seem only to report events must take steps to develop and to project an on-stage identity if they are to acquire and retain an audience:

> All presenters have to create a fictional persona which is close enough to the truth for them to feel comfortable and yet different enough for them to carry out the functions required of them without being shambolic.

(18)

Commenting upon this issue, Brodie (2008) makes it plain that stand-up comedians must construct an identity if their narrative reflections are to secure an appropriate audience response. Thus Brodie insists that stand-up comedians must locate their humour within a performed biography as they work to secure the audience affiliation necessary to co-construct humour and to precipitate laughter.

Comedians have, it seems, a number of short-hand phrases which neatly capture this understanding that the on-stage identity adopted by the performer is a concoction and affectation. Reflecting the Jewish roots of the most famous comedians of the last century, this is often condensed to one word: *shtick*.

In this context *shtick* has two meanings. Firstly *shtick* refers to the performer's 'routine'; the riffs, stories and repeated refrains which act as nests for the humorous projections uttered. The importance of such repertoires is largely overlooked by Greatbatch and Clark (2005). This omission occurs, I suggest, because the data-set developed by the authors tends to rob the performer of a biography while producing a decontextualised account of the performance event. In contrast, the re-framed account of guru performance outlined here, would, I suggest, recognise the importance of *shtick* and, in recognising the riffs and routines that are characteristic of comedy performance, would enable a more fully contextualised appreciation of *what gurus say*.

Secondly *shtick* highlights the efforts which the performer of stand-up comedy must make to craft and to sustain the identity necessary to allow him/her, for example, to appear plausibly as angry, misanthropic, sexually voracious or just 'a sicko'. This is, of course, a brief yet far from exhaustive listing of the identities available to stand-up comedians. Furthermore, we must acknowledge that the identities available to the guru performer are rather more constrained. Nonetheless, it seems sensible to suggest that to generate a pleasurable performance experience, the guru performer must be, like the stand-up comedian, somehow larger, better and/or more personable than the solitary individual who served the corporation or who completed hundreds of hours of advanced study.

This recognition of the identity-work necessary to cause and allow stand-up comedy suggests that we should, if we are to honour the guru seminar as a performance within an extend chain of events, look for and consider seriously the manner in which the gurus have been obliged to take steps to cultivate public personae. An element of this inquiry, as we shall discuss next, might usefully consider the disclosures made by the gurus when they appear before us.

Disclosure

Comics perform their *shtick* and reveal their public personae to us through projections of humour (of course) and through public declarations and disclosures. The Scots comedian Frankie Boyle, for example, offers declarations and disclosures which project a *sicko* identity, albeit one that is intelligent and politically-informed. Not all comedians, of course, may be so neatly pigeon-holed and plainly those who simply crack jokes tend to make fewer disclosures than those who nest their humorous projections within broader reflections and observations. Yet all performers do tell us something about themselves, deliberately or otherwise. This recognition of the role which disclosures perform in the construction and maintenance of the performer's identity suggests that we need to reflect further upon the utterances and, more broadly, the projections made by the guru performers. Greatbatch and Clark (2005), of course, are not unaware of this. They observe, for example, the manner in which management's gurus construct and project forms of talk designed to highlight their competence, experience and credibility. Indeed, in chapter five we highlighted the manner in which the story preferences observed by the authors might now be understood as disclosures directed towards the audience and to others such as agents and editors. Yet as we attempt to reframe guru performance there is, I suggest, a need to develop a more thorough exploration and analytical appreciation of such disclosures.

Taking Tom Peters as our example it is, perhaps, worth observing that this performer now routinely discloses his age (he was born in 1942) and uses this disclosure, I suggest, to establish both his primacy and his longevity as a guru. Yet perhaps more importantly, this disclosure may be read as an attempt to project this performer's identity as someone who cares little for orthodox ideas and preference or indeed the opprobrium of others (who may not be ready to accept the essential truth of his manifesto). In a seminar which took place in the London Hilton Metropole Hotel in 2004, for example, Peters offers the following disclosure a mere 50 seconds into a day-long seminar:[1]

> One of the joys: there are some things about being sixty-one which are not joyful=aches and pains which are part of the act uh there are some things which are quite joyful, the most significant one being that you are not interested in being invited back anywhere therefore you speak your mind and uh (0.5) that's exactly what I intend to do.

In a similar vein it is worth noting that Anthony Robbins, while encouraging his audience to take charge of their lives and to develop new habits that will enable their goals, chooses to disclose his own troubled childhood and his early estrangement from his parents. This form of disclosure (made, for example, in the *Unlimited Power* audio-tape which was published by Simon and Schuster in 1986[2]), I suggest, might be read as one of the persuasive examples which Lischinsky (2008) suggests is central to the representational work undertaken by the gurus. In this context, the disclosures made by Robbins might be examined as a case study where the speaker (re)presents himself as a visible, living, breathing and affluent manifestation of the validity of the manifesto which the audience has gathered to hear.

This reference to the audience 'gathering' reminds us, of course, that guru seminars are live events and that there is a need, therefore, to acknowledge the extent to which we continue to valorise the live event.

Liveness

Commenting upon the appeal of the live guru performance, Greatbatch and Clark (2005) suggest that these events attract audiences because they develop a) a sense of community and b) allow feelings of superiority over those who, for whatever reason, have failed to secure entry to the auditorium. This is, we should concede, a perfectly plausible rationalisation of the audience's motivations.

Yet this account of the attractions of the live event does tend to indulge an account of performance that is both nostalgic and ahistoric. Exploring these issues, Auslander (2008) observes that accounts of performance proceed from an ontology of liveness which asserts that live performance is an authentic non-reproducible singular moment in time defined by its vanishing, evanescent quality. Quoting Phelan (1993: 149), Auslander (2008) observes:

> Performance honours the idea that a limited number of people in a specific time/space can have an experience of value which leaves no visible trace afterwards.

(41)

Auslander protests, however, that this ontology is unhelpful. Televisual images, he reminds us, flicker and vanish 50 times per second. Similarly, recordings stored upon ferro-magnetic media change and decay such that each time we press 'play', the experience will be unique. Building upon this technological account of recording and reproduction, Auslander adds further objections to our common-sense valorisation of performance. The concept of 'liveness', he warns us, is effectively meaningless until that point in history when we develop the capability to apprehend live events. Indeed, he argues that when it comes to music, our test of authenticity is generally founded upon a comparison between the live event and the studio recording which precedes it! Furthermore, he points out that those who assume that a sense of community develops only within the moment of the live performance event fail to appreciate that 'rave culture' and before this, the disco scene, were both built upon recordings. Nonetheless, Auslander concedes that there is symbolic capital associated with 'the live' which sustains its societal valorisation. Performers across all genres recognise and understand this valorisation. They understand that as the lights go down in the auditorium, the audience expects and demands something novel; something unique. Perhaps the most obvious way to cultivate this impression is for the performer to suggest and/or enact some degree of spontaneity. Performers involved in pantomime, for example, understand this only too well. Pantomime directors, therefore, will carefully script and stage sections of performance which have been designed to appear impromptu. Thus actors in pantomime will, night after night, deliver scripted lines that are, apparently, 'off-the-cuff'. Indeed, actors in this form of theatre will *practice* trips, falls and 'prop malfunctions' in the sure and certain knowledge that audiences find these seemingly spontaneous cock-ups to be both funny and meaningful.

Tom Peters is, it seems, very conscious that his audiences valorise 'liveness'. His conduct reflects a very clear understanding that audiences expect and demand both novelty and spontaneity from his seminar gatherings.

Recognising the manner in which 'liveness' is constituted and validated by the audience, Peters, for example, claims continuously to revise and to update the visual aids which illuminate his presentations, even as he is touring.[3] At the start of the presentation that he delivered to the Peacock Theatre on the afternoon of September 3, 2009, for example, Peters informs his audience that this event is part of a speaking tour. He tells his London audience that on September 1st he offered a seminar on business excellence to the people of Glasgow. Furthermore, he adds that on September 2nd he hosted a similar event in Manchester. Indeed, he tells those present that on the morning of September 3rd he offered a seminar on business excellence specifically tailored to the challenges facing human resource professionals. Yet Peters is at pains to point out that the audience present for this afternoon event will experience a seminar that captures the very latest developments in his thinking. Thus he offers the following remarks as he embarks upon his performance:

Peacock Theatre 00:08:22

Let me, let me give you a footnote about this presentation. Uh. You're getting number three in line, this morning was slightly different, to a different group of people, but it's uh more specialised for Human Resource people. Uh. You're getting presentation number three out of three, which may (5) suggest staleness on the one hand, what it actually suggests is that (5) at (20) some time between 11 o'clock and midnight last night I decided that I wasn't happy with what I had done the prior two da::ys and from midnight until *five o'clock* I rewrote what I had done in Manchester and what I had done in Glasgow uh and to re (5) put-it-together in a slightly different fashion. So one of the things may mean, given that it was midnight-to-five there could be, despite the squiggly lines, a typographical error here or there for which I will apologise in advance.

Repair

Academics and journalists have often portrayed management's gurus as rather special individuals who retain, seemingly, an unrivalled capacity to control the thoughts and actions of practitioners. Greatbatch and Clark (2005), of course, challenge this account to some degree. Their reflections upon performance make it plain that the guru remains dependent upon his/her audience and must be careful to enrol those present. And yet the data reproduced by Greatbatch and Clark seems to assume that audience enrolment, while problematic in principle, generally runs smoothly for the management guru. Indeed, the materials reproduced by Greatbatch and Clark tend to indulge the assumption that the guru-performer never misreads the audience nor over-steps the boundaries established by his/her discourse community.

The conduct of stand-up comedians offers a useful contrast to this pre-sumption and, consequently, a provocation to think more carefully about the active processes of 'repair' which often need to be invoked in the name of audience management. In this regard, it is worth drawing attention to the *'too soon?'* question/motif often invoked by comedians.

The *'too soon?'* question/motif tends to be voiced when the stand-up comedian's projection of humour in the context of a recent and tragic event, for example, causes the audience to groan or to wince rather than laugh. At this point in time the question *'too soon?'* needs to be read as a challenge rather than as an innocent inquiry. Indeed, it is worth noting that the question when posed (often in an exaggerated and mocking tone) may be understood as a form of 'repair' insofar as the audience, when challenged in this way, will respond with laughter. This laughter, we should acknowledge, takes place *with* the comedian, but it is the audience that is the target. Indeed, it is worth pointing out that variants of the *'too soon?'* question will often reproach the audience for laughing at a previous (and similarly problematic) utterance while apparently refusing to accept the most recent projection as a humorous episode.

Some comedians (Stuart Lee (2010) springs to mind), for example, seem to make 'repair' a central component of their routines. Indeed, Lee pro-tests that he will often set out deliberately to alienate his audience so that he might then enjoy the personal satisfaction that follows the successful re-enrolment of this apparently wholly disaffected discourse community. In comparison, management's gurus seem altogether more conservative in their interactions. And yet it seems sensible to suggest that if we are, truly, to conceive of the guru seminar as an ongoing interaction, we should allow and look for those moments when the continuing enrolment of the guru's audience is threatened and/or in doubt. Again, an example drawn from the performance artistry of Tom Peters should serve to illustrate this dynamic *and* provide a prompt for further research and reflection.

During a seminar event (hosted by the London Business Forum and held in The Brewery in London on March 17, 2005)[4] which saw Peters 'matched' against Richard Scase in 'The Fight for Competitive Advantage', Peters mis-quotes *The Little Prince* (de Saint-Exupéry, [1943] 1995). Peters seems to regard this (mis)quotation as a very pithy and pertinent reflection on the central problem of managerial leadership. Yet this projection leaves the audience unmoved.

At first Peters struggles openly with this unexpected outcome. Yet in the following moments as he works to process the initial failure of his utterance, Peters is able to effect a repair. The completeness of this repair, of course, may be open to question. Nevertheless, the 'repair' activity undertaken by Peters in the extract reproduced here does at least allow the speaker to move on with his argument in a manner that prevents a more serious or more permanent divide from emerging.

The Brewery (disc two) 02:34

In The Little Prince=I love this quote, Richard=I don't know what you'll think of this quote. I think it's very schmaltzy but I love it.

If you want to build a ship=now think about this in terms of your 10 or 20 or 50 person organisation=if you want to build a ship don't drum up people together to collect wood and don't assign tasks and work but rather teach them to long for the sea.

Does that do er you're not reacting at all.

L-L-L

I mean that does a lot for me. That is the point is not to organise the work effectively it is to cause people to want to do something special. And if they really want to do something special then fundamentally they'll figure out how to organise themselves.

Isn't that what he's saying?

Yeh, I mean, yeh. It's cool right?

I mean the reaction is *like zero.*

L-L-L

Right so I liked it you didn't

L-L-L

You're not reacting at all?

Do you have a problem with this?

L-L-L

It doesn't do anything for you?

It doesn't?

L-L-L

No. But the point is=you see the point?

I I don't wanna tell them to put boards together to make a bo:at.

I want them to desperately want to get from where they are in South East Asia to Polynesian Islands. Right?

But isn't that what we want to do with the accounting department and the purchasing department?

It's not that what we wanna organise the work better it's that we want to have people in logistics imagine that they could be as effective as Dell or Tesco. Right?

We want them to long for the sea.
OK. Well I tried. *I did.* I tried my best. I'm usually pretty good. So that didn't work.
L-L-L
So. Maybe you can deal with simple English . . .
L-L-L

Concluding comments

Taken together, chapters five and six have offered an analysis of the nature and practices of guru theorising. Reviewing the academic literature on guru performance, we have acknowledged the pioneering contributions made by Clark and Greatbatch (2002, 2003; Greatbatch and Clark, 2003, 2005). The papers produced by this partnership now constitute academic understanding of *what gurus do*. We have however attempted to challenge this orthodoxy.

We have argued that the analyses of guru performance produced by Clark and Greatbatch are flawed:

1   Conceptually, because they fail to develop a useful and stable conceptualisation of the guru performer that is rooted empirically and supportive of empirical inquiry.
2   Methodologically, because they reject and yet require a model of storytelling that they have dismissed as *a priori* and so determinist.
3   Empirically, because their preferred account of storytelling fails to acknowledge the manner in which their limited data-set produces truth-claims that are, variously, exaggerated and/or rendered in a decontextualised manner.

In an attempt to overcome these limitations, we have invited a reanalysis of *what gurus do*, which is situated within a more developed appreciation of the nature and processes of performance. Building upon Schechner's reflections on identity, co-production and constrained freedom within the performance context, we have argued that there are affinities between *what gurus do* and the performances offered by stand-up comics which are worthy of further empirical analysis. In an attempt to bring order to this provocation, we have considered the manner in which the valorisation of liveness in comedy combined with an account of disclosures, identity-work and repair strategies suggest new avenues for research.

Within this broad attempt to reframe understanding of guru performance, there are clearly opportunities to pursue particular threads and/or more dedicated lines of inquiry. In closing, therefore, I suggest two avenues of inquiry that might now be considered within this frame.

My first suggestion for further research is based upon an acknowledgement that in (mainstream) show-business, would-be female comedians have often struggled to be regarded as funny, and so, commercially viable. Given the male-dominated nature of guru theory, it seems sensible to suggest that we might now take steps to consider the experience of female performers on the lecture-circuit:

• What forms of identity are available to/negotiated by these performers?
• Are the disclosures voiced by such performers more constrained than those of their male counterparts?
• And in this context do female gurus struggle? Personally, with 'authenticity'?

My second suggestion, while acknowledging the potential for gender stereotyping, invites analysis of the manner in which gurus develop their craft as performers. The biographies of stand-up comedians (see for example Kind, 2011) generally detail a pecking order of performers and a hierarchy of engagements; a progression from free to paid work; from short to long 'spots'; from opening act to headliner; from one-off booking to national tour. Given this, it seems sensible to suggest that we might now take time to reflect upon the manner in which our gurus are 'discovered', nurtured, packaged and presented. Clark and Greatbatch (2003) have, of course, touched upon a portion of this insofar as they acknowledge the extent to which the gurus lean upon the services (and goodwill) of their publishers and editors. I suggest that there is now an opportunity to consider the manner in which the gurus are launched and packaged as performers. In short: Is there a circuit for the would-be guru? Is there, as there is for the comedian, a well-trodden career path? And if so, are there key gate-keepers whom we might enrol in future research?

And finally . . . we should take a moment to make it plain that our assertion that guru performances and those offered by stand-up comedians have affinities that are worthy of further reflection, such that the empirical analysis will offer productive insights which alter and advance academic appreciation, should not be read as suggesting that we can, in any sense, freeze our understanding of such gatherings. Live performance and our understanding of the nature, processes and virtues of live performance are, as Auslander (2008: 46) notes, 'but an historically contingent effect of their culturally determined uses'. In this regard, our attempt to reframe guru performance in and through the lens of stand-up comedy requires that we acknowledge the emerging practices of stand-up comedy and the spectrum of opportunities available to all those who would build new worlds in our name. To suggest that guru performance and stand-up comedy have similarities and to suggest that further empirical research should be conducted to explore such affinities, therefore, is to acknowledge the continuing development of both art forms. Furthermore, this contingent appreciation must, at least, allow for the possibility of subsequent divergence in performance practices and effects. Such movements, divergent or otherwise, of course, may be revealed only in and through research which is based upon a clear-headed conceptualisation of guru performance and a robust and reliable methodology which can recognise and account for the dynamics of such gatherings *in situ*. These facets this little book has attempted to inscribe.

Notes

1 A recording of this event is available from Red Audio.
2 I am here referring to *Unlimited Power*, an audio-tape recording of an Anthony Robbins seminar which was published by Audioworks, a division of Simon and Schuster, in 1986.
3 Different iterations of Peters' presentations may be found at www.tompeters.com.
4 A recording is available from Red Audio.

Bibliography

Abrahamson E (1991) 'Managerial Fads and Fashions: The Diffusion and Rejection of Innovations', *Academy of Management Review*, 16 (3): 586–612.

Abrahamson E (1996) 'Management Fashion', *Academy of Management Review*, 21 (1): 254–285.

Anonymous A (1999) 'Confessions of a Ghost', *Inc.com*, http://pf.inc.com/magazine/19990515/4708.html

Atkinson J M and Heritage J (1984) *Structures of Social Action: Studies in Conversation Analysis*, Cambridge: Cambridge University Press.

Aupperle K E, Acar W and Booth D E (1986) 'An Empirical Critique of *In Search of Excellence*: How Excellent are the Excellent Companies?', *Journal of Management*, 12 (4): 499–512.

Auslander P (2008) *Liveness: Performance in a Mediatised Culture*, 2nd edition, Routledge: London and New York.

Baring-Gould S A (1914) *The Lives of the Saints*, John Grant: Edinburgh.

Barley S R and Kunda G (1992) 'Design and Devotion', *Administrative Science Quarterly*, 37: 363–399.

Baskerville S and Willett R (eds.) (1985) *Nothing Else to Fear: New Perspectives on America in the Thirties*, Manchester University Press: Manchester.

Bennett S (1997) *Theatre Audiences: A Theory of Production and Reception*, 2nd edition, Routledge: London and New York.

Boje D (1991) 'The Storytelling Organization: A Study of Performance in an Office Supply Firm', *Administrative Science Quarterly*, 36: 106–126.

Boje D (2001) *Narrative Methods for Organizational and Communication Research*, Sage: London.

Boltanski L and Chiapello E (2007) *The New Spirit of Capitalism*, Translated by G Elliot, Verso: London.

Boulting N (2011) *How I Won the Yellow Jersey: Dispatches from the Tour de France*, Yellow Jersey Press: London.

Branson R (1998) *Losing My Virginity: The Autobiography*, Random House: London.

Braverman H (1974) *Labor and Monopoly Capital*, Free Press: New York.

Brindle M and Stearns P (2001) *Facing Up to Management Faddism: A New Look at an Old Force*, Quorum Books: Westport, CT.

Brodie I (2008) 'Stand-Up Comedy as a Genre of Intimacy', *Ethnologies*, 3 (2): 153–180.

Bryan Y (2009) *Management Education in England: The Urwick Report*, Unpublished Thesis submitted to the University of Exeter for the degree: Doctor of Education.

Burnes B (2004) 'Kurt Lewin and the Planned Approach to Change: A Re-Appraisal', *Journal of Management Studies*, 41 (6): 977–1002.

Burrell G (1997) *Pandemonium*, Sage: London.

Butler N and Stoyanova-Russell D (2018) 'No Funny Business: Precarious Work and Emotional Labour in Stand-Up Comedy', *Human Relations*, 71 (12).

Carroll D T (1983) 'A Disappointing Search for Excellence', *Harvard Business Review*, November–December: 78–82.

Chandler A (1962) *Strategy and Structure: Chapters in the History of the Industrial Enterprise*, MIT Press: Cambridge, MA.

Clark T (2004) 'The Fashion of Management Fashion: A Surge Too Far?', *Organization*, 11 (2): 297–306.

Clark T and Greatbatch D (2002) 'Knowledge Legitimation and Affiliation through Storytelling: The Example of Management Gurus', in Clark T and Fincham (eds.) *Critical Consulting: New Perspectives on the Management Advice Industry*, Blackwell: Oxford.

Clark T and Greatbatch D (2003) 'Collaborative Relationships in the Creation and Fashioning of Management Ideas: Gurus, Editors and Managers', in Kipping M and Engwall L (eds.) *Management Consulting: Emergence and Dynamics of a Knowledge Industry*, Oxford University Press: Oxford.

Cole R E (1999) *Managing Quality Fads: How American Business Learned to Play the Quality Game*, Oxford University Press: Oxford.

Collins C and McCartney G (2010) 'TINA Is Back', in MacDonald D (ed.) *Scottish Review: The Anthology*, ICS Books: Kilmarnock.

Collins D (1994) 'The Disempowering Logic of Empowerment', *Empowerment in Organizations*, 2 (2): 14–21.

Collins D (1996) 'No Such Thing as a Practical Approach to Management', *Management Decision*, 34 (1): 66–71.

Collins D (1997) 'Knowledge Work of Working: Ambiguity and Confusion in the Analysis of the Knowledge Age', *Employee Relations*, 19 (1): 53–68.

Collins D (1998) *Organizational Change: Sociological Perspectives*, Routledge: London.

Collins D (2000) *Management Fads and Buzzwords: Critical-Practical Perspectives*, Routledge: London.

Collins D (2001) 'The Fad Motif in Management Scholarship', *Employee Relations*, 23 (1): 26–37.

Collins D (2003) 'Guest Editor's Introduction: Re-imagining Change', *Tamara: Journal of Critical Postmodern Organization Science*, 2 (4): iv–xi.

Collins D (2004) 'Who Put the Con in Consultancy? Fads, Recipes and "Vodka Margarine"', *Human Relations*, 57 (5): 553–572.

Collins D (2007) *Narrating the Management Guru: In Search of Tom Peters*, Routledge: Abingdon, Oxon.

Collins D (2012a) 'Management Fads and Fashion', in Boje D, Burnes B and Hassard J (eds.) *The Routledge Companion to Organizational Change*, Taylor and Francis, Routledge: Abingdon, Oxon: 310–321.

Collins D (2012b) 'Women Roar: "The Women's Thing" in the Storywork of Tom Peters', *Organization*, 19 (4): 405–424.

Collins D (2015) 'Foreword', in Örtenblad A (ed.) *Handbook of Research on Management Ideas and Panaceas*, Edward Elger Publishing: Cheltenham, Gloucester.

Collins D (2016) 'Constituting Best Practice in Management Consulting', *Culture and Organization*, 22 (5): 409–429.

Collins D (2018) *Stories for Management Success: The Power of Talk in Organizations*, Taylor and Francis, Routledge: Abingdon, Oxon.

Collins D (2019) 'Management's Gurus', in Sturdy Λ, Heusinkveld S, Reay T and Strang D (eds.) *The Oxford Handbook of Management Ideas*, Oxford University Press: Oxford.

Comfort A (1972) *The Joy of Sex: A Gourmet Guide to Lovemaking*, Crown: London.

Cooke B, Wood T and Macau F (2012) 'Brazilian Management Gurus as Reflexive Soft-HRM Practitioners: An Empirical Study', *The International Journal of Human Resource Management*, 24 (1): 110–129.

Covey S (1989) *The Seven Habits of Highly Successful People*, Simon and Schuster: New York.

Crainer S (1997) *Corporate Man to Corporate Skunk: The Tom Peters Phenomenon: A Biography*, Capstone: Oxford.

Crainer S (1998a) *The Ultimate Business Guru Book: 50 Thinkers Who Made Management*, Capstone: Oxford.

Crainer S (1998b) 'In Search of the Real Author', *Management Today*, May: 50–54.

Davenport T, Prusak L and Wilson H J (2003) *What's the Big Idea? Creating and Capitalizing on the Best Management Thinking*, Harvard Business School Press: Boston, MA.

Deal T and Kennedy A (1982) *Corporate Cultures: The Rites and Rituals of Corporate Life*, Addison-Wesley: Reading, MA.

De la Tour A (2013) *Stand-Up or Die*, Oberon Books: London.

de Saint-Exupéry A [1943] (1995) *The Little Prince and Letter to a Hostage*, Translated by T V F Cuffe, Penguin Books: London.

Double O (2005) *Getting the Joke: The Inner Workings of Stand-Up Comedy*, Methuen: London.

Drucker P [1955] (2007) *The Effective Executive*, London and New York: Taylor and Francis, Routledge.

Dunford R and Palmer I (1996) 'Metaphors in Popular Management Discourse: The Case of Corporate Restructuring', in Grant D and Oswick C (eds.) *Metaphor and Organizations*, Sage: London and New York.

Dunlap A and Andelman B (1997) *Mean Business: How I Save Bad Companies and Make Good Companies Great*, Fireside: New York, NY.

Economist(The) (1994) 'Tom Peters, Performance Artist', September 24.

Edersheim E (2004) *McKinsey's Marvin Bower: Vision, Leadership and the Creation of Management Consulting*, John Wiley: Hoboken, NJ.

Eldridge J E T (1983) 'Review of Wood S (ed.) *The Degradation of Work?* And Littler C *The Development of the Labour Process in Capitalist Societies*', *British Journal of Industrial Relations*, 21 (3): 418–420.

Engwall L, Kipping M and Üsdiken B (eds.) (2016) *Defining Management: Business Schools, Consultants, Media*, Routledge: London.

Fixx J F (1977) *The Complete Book of Running*, Random House: New York.

Fox A (1985) *Man Mismanagement*, Hutchinson: London.

Furusten S (1999) *Popular Management Books: How They Are Made and What They Mean for Organizations*, London: Routledge.

Gabriel Y (2000) *Storytelling in Organizations: Facts, Fictions and Fantasies*, Oxford University Press: Oxford.

Geneen H and Moscow A (1986) *Managing*, Grafton Books: London.

Gioia D A and Chittipeddi K (1991) 'Sensemaking and Sensegiving in Strategic Change Initiation', *Strategic Management Journal*, 12: 433–448.

Giroux H (2006) 'It Was Such a Handy Term: Management Fashions and Pragmatic Ambiguity', *Journal of Management Studies*, 43 (6): 1227–1260.

Goffman E (1959) *The Presentation of Self in Everyday Life*, Doubleday: London.

Grant D and Oswick C (1996) 'Introduction: Getting the Measure of Metaphors', in Grant D and Oswick C (eds.) *Metaphor and Organizations*, Sage: London and New York.

Gray J (1999) *False Dawn: The Delusions of Global Capitalism*, Granta: London.

Greatbatch D and Clark T (2003) 'Displaying Group Cohesiveness: Humour and Laughter in the Public Lectures of Management Gurus', *Human Relations*, 56 (12): 1515–1544.

Greatbatch D and Clark T (2005) *Management Speak: Why We Listen to What Management Gurus Tell Us*, Routledge: London.

Grint K (1994) 'Reengineering History: Social Resonances and Business Process Reengineering', *Organization*, 1 (1): 179–201.

Grint K (1997a) *Fuzzy Management*, Oxford University Press: Oxford.

Grint K (1997b) 'TQM, BPR, JIT, BSCs and TLAs: Managerial Waves or Drownings?', *Management Decision*, 35 (10): 731–738.

Groß C, Heusinkveld S and Clark T (2015) 'The Active Audience? Gurus, Management Ideas and Consumer Variability', *British Journal of Management*, 26 (2): 273–291.

Guerrier Y and Gilbert D (1995) 'The Role of Presentation Techniques in Selling Management Ideas through the "Heart" Not the Mind', Paper presented at 12th EGOS Colloquium, Istanbul.

Guest D (1992) 'Right Enough to Be Dangerously Wrong: An Analysis of the *In Search of Excellence* Phenomenon', in Salaman G (ed.) *Human Resource Strategies*, Sage: London.

Hammer M (1990) 'Re-Engineering Work: Don't Automate Obliterate', *Harvard Business Review*, July–August: 104–112.

Hayes R and Abernathy W (1980) 'Managing Our Way to Economic Decline', *Harvard Business Review*, July/August.

Hilmer F and Donaldson L (1996) *Management Redeemed: Debunking the Fads That Undermine Our Corporations*, Free Press: New York, NY.

Hindle T (2008) *Guide to Management Ideas and Gurus*, The Economist in Association with Profile Books: London.

Höpfl H (2005) 'The Organisation and the Mouth of Hell', *Culture and Organization*, 11 (3): 167–179.

Huczynski A A (1993) *Management Gurus: What Makes Them and How to Become One*, Routledge: London.

Hyatt J (1999) 'When Everyone Was Excellent', *Inc.com*, http://pf.inc.com/magazine/19990515/4703.html

Iacocca L and Kleinfield S (1988) *Talking Straight*, Bantam Books: New York, NY.

Iacocca L and Novak W (1984) *Iacocca*, Bantam Books: London.

Isaacson W (2011) *Steve Jobs*, Little-Brown: London.

Jackson B (1996) 'Re-Engineering the Sense of Self: The Manager and the Management Guru', *Journal of Management Studies*, 33 (5): 571–590.

Jackson B (2001) *Management Gurus and Management Fashions: A Dramatistic Inquiry*, Routledge: London.

Jackson N and Carter P (1998) 'Management Gurus and Management Fashions', in Hassard J and Holliday R (eds.) *Organization-Representation: Work and Organization in Popular Culture*, Sage: London.

Kahn H (1970) *The Emerging Japanese Superstate*, Harper and Row: London.

Kahn H and Pepper T (1978) *The Japanese Challenge: The Success and Failure of Economic Success*, Harper and Row: London.

Kanter R M (1989) *When Giants Learn to Dance*, Free Press: New York, NY.

Kennedy C [1991] (1996) *Managing with the Gurus: Top Level Guidance on 20 Management Techniques*, Century Books: London.

Kennedy C [1994] (1998) *Guide to the Management Gurus: Shortcuts to the Leading Ideas of Leading Management Thinkers*, 2nd edition, Century Books: London.

Kiam V (1988) *Keep Going for It: Living the Life of an Entrepreneur*, Harper Collins: New York, NY.

Kieser A (1997) 'Rhetoric and Myth in Management Fashion', *Organization*, 4 (1): 49–74.

Kind A (2011) *Stand Up and Deliver*, Monarch Books: Oxford.

Kipping M and Engwall L (eds.) (2003) *Management Consulting: Emergence and Dynamics of a Knowledge Industry*, Oxford University Press: Oxford.

Kociatkiewicz J and Kostera M (2016) 'Grand Plots of Management Bestsellers: Learning from Narrative and Thematic Coherence', *Management Learning*, 47 (3): 324–342.

Kondratieff N D (1935) 'The Long Waves in Economic Life', *Review of Economic Statistics*, (17): 105–115.

Kostera M (2015) *Occupy Management: Inspirations and Ideas for Self-Organization and Self-Management*, Routledge: Abingdon, Oxon.

Kuhrana R (2007) *From Higher Aims to Hired Hands: The Social Transformation of American Business Schools and the Unfilled Promise of Management as a Profession*, Princeton University Press: Princeton.

Latour B (1987) *Science in Action*, Harvard University Press: Cambridge, MA.

Lee S (2010) *How I Escaped My Certain Fate: The Life and Deaths of a Stand-Up Comedian*, Faber and Faber: London.

Lewin K (1947) 'Group Decisions and Social Change', in Macoby E E, Newcomb T M and Hartley E L (eds.) *Readings in Social Psychology*, Henry Holt: New York, NY.

Lischinsky A (2008) 'Examples as Persuasive Argument in Popular Management Literature', *Discourse and Communication*, 2 (3): 243–269.

Maidique M A (1983) 'Point of View: The New Management Thinkers', *California Management Review*, 26 (1): 151–161.

McInnes J (1989) *Thatcherism at Work*, Open University Press: Milton Keynes.

McKenna C D (2007) *The World's Newest Profession: Management Consulting in the Twentieth Century*, Cambridge University Press: Cambridge.

McKenna C D (2016) 'Writing the Ghost-Writer Back in: Alfred Sloan, Alfred Chandler, John McDonald and the Intellectual Origins of Corporate Strategy', *Management and Organizational History*, 1 (2): 107–126.

Micklethwait J and Wooldridge A (1997) *The Witch Doctors: What the Management Gurus Are Saying, and How to Make Sense of It*, Mandarin: London.

Mintz L E (1985) 'Standup Comedy as Social and Cultural Mediation', *American Quarterly*, 37 (1): 71–80.

Mitchell T R (1985) 'In Search of Excellence versus the 100 Best Companies to Work for in America: A Question of Perspective and Values', *The Academy of Management Review*, 10 (2): 350–355.

Morgan G (1986) *Images of Organization*, Sage: London.

Niven D (1971) *The Moon's a Balloon*, Hamish Hamilton: London.

Oliver N (1990) 'Just-in-Time: The New Religion of Western Manufacturing', Proceedings of the British Academy of Management Conference, Glasgow, UK.

Pagel S and Westerfelhaus R (2005) 'Charting Managerial Reading Preferences in Relation to Popular Management Theory Books: A Semiotic Analysis', *Journal of Business Communication*, 42: 420–448.

Parker M (2018) *Shut Down the Business School: What's Wrong with Management Education*, Pluto Press: London.

Pascale R and Athos A (1981) *The Art of Japanese Management*, Sidgwick and Jackson: London.

Pattison S (1997) *The Faith of the Managers: When Management Becomes Religion*, Cassell: London.

Peters T (1987) *Thriving on Chaos: Handbook for a Management Revolution*, Guild Publishing: London.

Peters T (1994) *The Pursuit of Wow! Every Person's Guide to Topsy Turvy Times*, MacMillan: London.

Peters T and Austin N (1985) *A Passion for Excellence: The Leadership Difference*, Fontana: London.

Peters T and Waterman R (1982) *In Search of Excellence: Lessons from America's Best Run Companies*, Harper and Row: New York.

Phelan P (1993) *Unmarked: The Politics of Performance*, London and New York: Routledge.

Pinder C C and Bourgeois V W (1982) 'Controlling Tropes in Administrative Science', *Administrative Science Quarterly*, 27 (4): 641–652.

Pio E (2007) 'Gurus and Indian Epistemologies: Parables of Labor-Intensive Organizations', *Journal of Management Inquiry*, 16 (2): 180–192.

Rigby R (2011) *28 Business Thinkers Who Changed the World: The Management Gurus and Mavericks Who Changed the Way We Think about Business*, Kogan Page: London.

Ritzer G (2004) *The Globalization of Nothing*, London: Pine Forge Press.

Roddick A (1991) *Body and Soul: How to Succeed in Business and Change the World*, Elbury Press: London.

Roddick A (2005) *Business as Usual: My Entrepreneurial Journey: Profits and Principles*, Anita Robbick Books: London.

Roy K (2013) *The Invisible Spirit: A Life of Post-War Scotland, 1945–75*, Birlinn Ltd: Edinburgh.

Rüling C C (2005) 'Popular Concepts and the Business Management Press', *Scandinavian Journal of Management*, 21: 177–195.

Sampson A (1973) *The Sovereign State: The Secret History of ITT*, Hodder and Stoughton: London.

Sampson A [1975] (1991) *The Seven Sisters: The Great Oil Companies and the World They Made*, Bantam Books: London.

Sampson A (1977) *The Arms Bazaar: From Lebanon to Lockheed*, The Viking Press: New York.

Schechner R [1977] (2003) *Performance Theory*, Routledge: London and New York.

Schein E (1985) *Organizational Culture and Leadership*, Jossey-Bass: San Francisco.

Semler R (1994) *Maverick: The Success Story Behind the World's Most Unusual Workplace*, Arrow Books: London.

Senge P (1990) *The Fifth Discipline*, Doubleday: New York.

Sharpe T (1984) 'The Day I Saw John Fenton or "By the inch it's a cinch"', *Management Education and Development*, 15 (1): 14–16.

Sloan A P, McDonald J and Stevens C (1965) *My Years with General Motors*, Doubleday and Company: New York.

Suddaby R and Greenwood R (2001) 'Colonizing Knowledge: Commodification as a Dynamic of Jurisdictional Expansion in Service Firms', *Human Relations*, 54 (7): 933–953.

Taylor F W (1911) *The Principles of Scientific Management*, Harper and Row: New York.

Thomas P (1999) *Fashions in Management Research: An Empirical Analysis*, Ashgate: Aldershot.

Van der Merwe R and Pitt L (2003) 'Are Excellent Companies Ethical? Evidence from an Industrial Setting', *Corporate Reputation Review*, 5 (4): 343–355.

Veblen T (1994) *The Theory of the Leisure Class*, Dover Publications: ON, Canada.

Watson T (2001) *In Search of Management: Culture, Chaos and Control in Managerial Work*, Thomson Learning: London.

Weick K (1995) *Sensemaking in Organizations*, Sage: London.

Weick K (2004) 'A Bias for Conversation: Acting Discursively in Organizations', in Grant D, Hardy C, Oswick C and Putnam L (eds.) *The Sage Handbook of Organizational Discourse*, Sage: London and New York.

Welch J and Byrne J (2001) *Jack: What I've Learned Leading a Great Company and Great People*, Headline Publishing: London.

Westwood R (2007) 'The Staging of Humour: Organizing and Managing Comedy', in Westwood R and Rhodes C (eds.) *Humour, Work and Organization*, Routledge: London.

Wolfe T (1979) *The Right Stuff*, Jonathan Cape: London.

Woodward B and Bernstein C (1974) *All the President's Men*, Simon and Schuster: New York.

Index

Note: Page numbers in *italics* indicate figures on the corresponding page.